The Prism of Truth

The Prism of Truth

Reflections on Myth

ANTHONY O'HEAR

CASCADE *Books* • Eugene, Oregon

THE PRISM OF TRUTH
Reflections on Myth

Copyright © 2024 Anthony O'Hear. All rights reserved. Except for brief quotations in critical publications or reviews, no part of this book may be reproduced in any manner without prior written permission from the publisher. Write: Permissions, Wipf and Stock Publishers, 199 W. 8th Ave., Suite 3, Eugene, OR 97401.

Cascade Books
An Imprint of Wipf and Stock Publishers
199 W. 8th Ave., Suite 3
Eugene, OR 97401

www.wipfandstock.com

PAPERBACK ISBN: 978-1-6667-8101-4
HARDCOVER ISBN: 978-1-6667-8102-1
EBOOK ISBN: 978-1-6667-8103-8

Cataloguing-in-Publication data:

Names: O'Hear, Anthony [author].

Title: The prism of truth : reflections on myth / Anthony O'Hear.

Description: Eugene, OR: Cascade Books, 2024 | Includes bibliographical references and index.

Identifiers: ISBN 978-1-6667-8101-4 (paperback) | ISBN 978-1-6667-8102-1 (hardcover) | ISBN 978-1-6667-8103-8 (ebook)

Subjects: LCSH: Myth. | Mythology. | Science and religion. | Religion—Philosophy. | God. | Religion.

Classification: BL313 O34 2024 (print) | BL313 (ebook)

VERSION NUMBER 100824

To Natasha, Jacob, and Thea,
with love and admiration

Contents

Preface | ix

Introduction | 1

1 Not the End of the Matter: Wittgenstein and the Limits of Scientific Discourse | 6

2 The Place of Myth in Human Life | 24

3 Addison's Walk: A Story of Two Mythologists | 49

4 From Myth to Science: A Popperian Analysis | 57

5 A Storied World | 71

6 A Plenitude of Myths | 87

7 A Florentine Story: Christian Platonism in the Renaissance | 114

Bibliography | 133
Index | 139

Preface

I AM GRATEFUL TO a number of people who in various ways have contributed ideas and thoughts to this book. I presented a very early version of the first part of the book at the Oxford University Theology Faculty's Work in Progress meeting in February 2022. Mark Wynn, Dave Leal, Tim Mawson, and Richard Swinburne were all very helpful there. In September 2023 I spoke on the same material at the meeting convened in Trogir, Croatia, by the Humane Philosophy Society and the Ian Ramsey Centre. Andrew Pinsent was particularly helpful there, as were Ralph Weir, Samuel Hughes, and Mikolaj Slawkowski-Rode. Alan Montefiore kindly read and commented on an early draft of some of the material, while at different times I was helped in different ways by Jordan Peterson, Douglas Hedley, Perry Marshall, Esmé Partridge (on Herbert of Cherbury), Natasha O'Hear, A. N. Wilson, Alan Bekhor, Zdzisław Mach and John Cottingham. I was helped by Hazhir Teimourian, with his thoughts on the Ultimate, and on Islamic thought, by Fitzroy Morrissey.

I owe a particular debt to Charles Taliaferro not only for his thoughts on the topic, but also for introducing me to Robin Parry at Cascade and Wipf and Stock. And I am immeasurably grateful to Robin for his wonderful commenting, editing, and support throughout.

Introduction

ACCORDING TO MANY RELIGIOUS traditions, God, or some uncreated and transcendent Being, is the creator and sustainer of the whole cosmos, including our own world. But, given the ontological and epistemological abyss that would separate such a Being from us and our understanding, how can we humans gain knowledge of this "Being beyond being"? Such a Being will, of necessity, be beyond our normal everyday concepts and our powers of comprehension; of necessity, because if we could describe it adequately in our human terms, it would be no more than a very powerful version of things we do know and have experience of. It would, as theologians and philosophers from many traditions testify, be no more than a being among beings, itself subject to all the types of question we naturally pose regarding things in our world. However powerful and wonderful, it would not be the ultimate reality beyond all the things of which we can gain direct knowledge. It would be subject to the same questions we ask about non-ultimate beings, questions about its cause, or about its goodness and its beauty, and so on. This humanly describable being among beings would not be the uncreated source of these realities. Its properties, whatever they were, would themselves need further explanation, and raise the same questions we would have about a non-ultimate reality. God is necessarily infinitely distant from us, and God's ways will not, in any straightforward way, be our ways.

One historically influential way of answering the question about how we can think about and refer to an ultimate God in human terms is to concede that while we have nothing other than human terms to use, we can use these terms in a *non-literal* way when referring to God. It is said that in this area we can use analogy or an analogical mode of speech, using our human language, but recognizing that we never completely capture or describe God by this means. The very words we use in this context cannot be understood in a literal way but should always be understood as mere pointers to what is beyond our comprehension and language. I do not want to question or reject the use of analogical language in theological discourse, but what I want to suggest in this book is that there is also a mythical way of approaching the divine.

Throughout history human societies and traditions have sustained and understood themselves by means of myths about divinity or divinities. In what follows I will argue against narrowly factual notions of truth and meaning. Myths, religious or not, are not by definition false. On the contrary, deep and otherwise unsuspected truths, inaccessible to scientific accounts of the world, are often conveyed in myths. It is only an over-literal understanding of the notion of truth that would immediately rule out an oblique approach to truth and to the divine through myths and stories.

Many of the most famous and influential myths in history have been myths about God or gods, locating human beings on a cosmic stage and of concern to, or at least of interest to, these divine beings. These will be religious myths, in other words. The very ubiquity and strength of such myths should give us pause before rejecting them all out of hand as mere fairy tales or wish fulfillment. At the very least we should be prepared to concede that they may be pointers to a realm and to truths beyond the everyday, to the ultimate source of all beings. One of the things I will do in this book is to explore some of the implications of taking religious myths as pointers to a transcendent super-human reality, indeed as revelations from that reality.

Examining what is implied in a widely encountered aspect of human cultures and traditions should be of interest even to those for whom this aspect of human life is considered to belong to a primitive, pre-rational phase of history. But, against so negative

INTRODUCTION

an attitude to religious myth, in the course of this book I will also suggest that we should be prepared to regard religious myths with at least a degree of favor, precisely because they tell us something about ourselves. They tell us about what seems to be a powerful and almost universal directedness of human thought and practice toward the transcendent. Should this pervasive facet of our mentality be rejected out of hand? May it not reveal to us something about ourselves? Is it inconceivable that these myths might convey to us something about the Being or beings from whom these mythical revelations are purported to come? That they could actually be revelations, in other words? I believe these questions to be important, and I want to leave them at least open in what follows.

Religious myths may, as in the case of Judaism, Christianity, and Islam, for example, be based on undoubted historical facts. But, as I will show, beyond the historically verifiable facts at the basis of these religions there is also a mythical understanding of those facts. As in other religious traditions, it is through this mythical level of understanding that we are taken out of this world and offered a religious understanding of it.

A key point in my argument is that because of the ineffability of the divine we have to approach it indirectly, not only through analogy or some other form of theological discourse, but also through myths. If the divine light shines on and in our world, myths could be seen as the prisms through which it reaches us. So, as I have just suggested, we should be prepared at least to entertain the thought that there could be elements of truth in the myths by which human beings have oriented themselves toward the divine, if only to see what might follow from such a concession. In doing so, we will learn something important about human nature and culture, and about what we are as individuals, even in a post-religious society. But if we take this road, regarding religious myths as important and worthy of study in and for themselves, given the way the divine is beyond human comprehension, we will also have to allow that no myth can be complete or final. No one of our myths can be more that a *partial* representation of *some* aspects of the divine ultimate.

Equally, against the temptation to wipe away the content of different myths in order to produce some syncretic amalgam of all myths, I will urge that we take the content of each one seriously. Each myth has its own specific way of approaching the realities it is dealing with, and to that extent has its own value. It has its own particular take on a transcendent reality that is many-faceted and contains multitudes, so to speak. Typically, indeed, the religious myths that have been most compelling to their human adherents have been ones in which what seem to us to be the tensions and contradictions within the divine are not so much resolved as held before us, the tension, for example between divine justice and divine mercy, or between divine goodness and evil in the world. By showing rather than by saying or telling, myths convey to us that we have to live these contrarieties, and how to live with them, without irritable searching for an intellectual "solution." But we will also have to admit that no human work is without blemish, and that there have been many occasions where religiously influential myths have, through understandable human attempts to tie down their meaning, degenerated into sources of superstition and hostility.

If one favored myth points to part of the truth, so will others, and even a favored myth may need reinterpretation and cleansing as time goes on. One of the themes I am interested in exploring in this book is occasions where adherents to one myth have also opened themselves to learning from other myths. Both cleansing of one's own tradition and charity to other traditions are possible; they have occurred in the past, and do so now. I hope that one conclusion to this book will be to encourage such developments, doubly important in a world where we are much more aware than earlier of competing claims and traditions jostling and rubbing up against each other in narrow-minded ways. Thinking about the transcendent and the nature of the myths that point to it should raise us above all that, leading us to cherish the myriad ways in which such revelations have emerged and developed through human history. As I say, we should be prepared to take seriously what these myths tell us about the orientation human beings seem

INTRODUCTION

naturally to have toward a more perfect world and Being beyond. There are, of course, myths which tell of no world beyond, but which eelaborate this-wordly fantasy or predict utopias in an earthly New Jerusalem. Examples of the latter will include the myths of Marxism and fascism, though these are not the only ones. Myths of worldly utopia and fantasy may have aspects in common with the the myths I am largely concerned with in this book, but in so far as they disavow any divine or transcendent source, they are fundamentally different in nature from them. I do though argue that one reason we should treat the apparently divinely inspired myths seriously is because of what they tell us about ourselves in this world. But I also hope that this book will encourage its readers to be sympathetic to the thought that these myths may also tell us something valuable about their ostensible *source*, the Being and the domain beyond, from which they appear to come and to which we are drawn.

1

Not the End of the Matter
Wittgenstein and the Limits of Scientific Discourse

A PREVALENT VIEW IN today's world is that science and scientific knowledge provide us with everything we need to know. On this view, for rational and thinking people, science has displaced earlier forms of thought, particularly the religious and the mythical. So, it would be claimed, even if scientific accounts as we have them at the moment are not complete, in principle everything about the world and indeed about us as human beings can and will be explained in scientific terms. Our everyday human talk about value is no more than an indirect way of working out how best to organize our lives so as to promote our naturally explicable urges to survive and reproduce, and in doing so to satisfy our equally natural instincts to maximize pleasure and minimize pain.

Broadly speaking much of twentieth-century philosophy, certainly in the English-speaking world, has attempted to develop this materialistic, quasi-scientific picture. In doing so it aims to eliminate appeals to anything not within the domain of the scientific. Elements of our language and practice that seem to go beyond the scientifically explicable will either be discarded altogether or explained away as being simply indirect ways of referring to the basic structures and processes revealed in science. In considering this story, a pivotal figure is the Viennese philosopher Ludwig Wittgenstein, who died in 1951 at the age of sixty-two. His early work was a hugely inspirational influence on what became known as logical positivism, a particularly forceful and influential statement of this scientific worldview. We will show in this chapter why Wittgenstein was seen in this way, but also why Wittgenstein's own view was never the reductively materialistic picture developed by the logical positivists and their still-influential philosophical successors.

Wittgenstein's early positivist readers, particularly in Vienna, could be forgiven for misunderstanding his intentions, but misunderstand him they did. Even more significant for our purposes, in the second half of his life Wittgenstein left Vienna for Cambridge. While there, Wittgenstein himself mounted what seems to those who follow him to be nothing less than a thoroughgoing demolition of the logical positivism that in his early days, and, perhaps despite his own intentions, he did so much to inspire. In what follows in this chapter, I will explain the story of the "two" Wittgensteins. I will also show why, even if many contemporary philosophers would not agree, to those who are prepared to follow him in his own personal journey, Wittgenstein's later demolition of scientistic philosophy is so convincing.

The early Wittgenstein, as we have already seen, did indeed propose a quasi-mathematical, scientific approach to reality, and also to language and meaning, which could indeed be encapsulated in a number of doctrines, in the manner of famous contemporaries of his, such as Bertrand Russell, Martin Heidegger, and Jean-Paul Sartre. But in the second half of his career he saw that philosophy, or perhaps better philosophizing or doing philosophy, was an intensely personal matter, something each of us has to work through for ourselves, and not reducible to a set of doctrines. In doing philosophy, one wrestled internally with the way one unthinkingly thought, which all too often is simply a case of reflecting the dominant ideas of one's time. Wittgenstein's aim became to see things right, to see things as they are, in a way uncontaminated by erroneous or superficial trends of thought, especially the trends of thought of one's own time to which one so easily and unthinkingly bends. But this letting the fly out of the fly-bottle, as he once put it, was an exercise each of us had to undertake for ourselves. It was *our* fly and *our* fly-bottle, or even *my* fly and *my* fly bottle. Philosophy of this nature could not be reduced to the ingestion of views or propositions laid down by another, however philosophically eminent they might be, even as eminent as Heidegger, Sartre, and Russell.

In his own philosophical investigation Wittgenstein embarked on a journey that took him from an unsparing insistence on the supremacy of scientific discourse over all others to a far richer and more humane sense of what we could know and say about ourselves, our minds, and the world. The *Tractatus Logico-Philosophicus* of 1921 was one of the only two works Wittgenstein published in his lifetime, the other being a comparatively unimportant lecture from 1929.[1] In the *Tractatus* Wittgenstein pronounced that apart from pure logic and empty tautologies deriving from the meanings of words, the only things that could legitimately be said were "propositions of natural science."[2] Meaningful talk about the world must consist of statements that pictured facts or states of affairs, in the sense that their own logical structure would mirror some possible fact or collection of such facts. The facts in question would be ones in which something definite was said of some identifiable object.

A preliminary way of looking at what Wittgenstein was proposing might be to take a simple state of affairs, such as the cat being on the mat, and the picturing proposition saying just that: "The cat is on the mat." But even if helpful as a way into Wittgenstein's notion of picturing, this would be misleading as any more than a very rough account of his analysis of language in the *Tractatus*.

---

1. Wittgenstein, *Tractatus Logico-Philosophicus* (originally *Logisch-Philosopische Abhandlung*, published 1921).

2. Wittgenstein, *Tractatus Logico-Philosophicus*, 151 (prop 6.53).

Not the End of the Matter

The *Tractatus*'s view of language and logic can be seen as mirroring the then-contemporary scientific approach to the physical world. According to the science of Wittgenstein's day, underneath the everyday appearances of the things with which we are all familiar there was a quite different and stranger universe. It did not consist of solid, unchanging, colored, tangible objects, but rather of tiny colorless particles separated by comparatively large areas of empty space in which they moved around at great speed. How the world appeared to us was due to the way these basic atoms (as they were thought of then) interacted with our brains and sense organs to give us the impression that the world was as it appeared to us, but underneath and *really* (as it would be said), things were quite different. For example, the real world is not colored or noisy or smelly—these and other experiences are somewhat misleadingly presented to us as if they belong to the world, but they are actually due to the way the colorless, silent, tasteless atoms interact with our sense organs so as to produce the illusions of color and the rest in our brains. But these so-called "secondary" qualities do not exist in the real world. They are produced by us, in our brains.

In our day the atoms of the early twentieth century have been transformed by quantum theory into far more spooky and peculiar entities, neither particles nor waves, and behaving in well-nigh unintelligible ways, but the principle is the same: a completely different world (and one still colorless, etc.) from what we see and experience constitutes the basic reality of the universe. Our own commonsense view, the world in which we live, gives us a highly misleading picture of reality, according to those who see the scientific picture as fundamental and our commonsense view as no more than a crutch to enable us to stumble around the world at our biologically superficial level.

In his analysis of language in the *Tractatus* Wittgenstein argued that for language to work and make sense it has to have an underlying structure again quite different from how it appeared on the surface. In order to secure its application to the world, central to language there had to be names that denoted or referred to objects, names that would be guaranteed to lock on to the objects they denoted. The objects on to which they locked would have to be, like the atoms of physics, simple and indivisible points that could not be further divided. Wittgenstein thus wanted far more basic facts or states of affairs than cats sitting on mats, and the elementary propositions describing these facts would simply consist of combinations of names. The objects constituting Wittgensteinian facts and named in the corresponding propositions would be simple atomic entities and the qualities they had, which were also absolutely primitive; and all these basic facts would be absolutely independent of each other. Wittgenstein never actually gave an example of such a basic fact, so it is hard to know exactly what they would consist in or what the relevant elementary propositions would say. His argument was built up from what he argued was necessary for language to function, for it to latch on to the world and make sense. To use another terminology, what he was attempting to do was to lay bare the conditions of possibility of language. Language exists, and works, but what must be true for this to be so? So, given that language does work, what makes it possible must also be true, and that, in Wittgenstein's early view, was given to us in his account of basic facts and the corresponding propositions describing those facts.

In laying out what makes language possible (in his view at the time), it is clear he was envisaging something like descriptions of the most basic and indivisible particles of science with whatever qualities they were allowed to have, with situations like the cat being on the mat being built up from complexes of such elementary facts, rather as the scientific worldview would have it. Language itself was now to be seen as being built up from underlying entities and structures radically different from how it appeared in everyday talk.

Wittgenstein's achievement in the *Tractatus*, following earlier pioneering work by Bertrand Russell, was to show how a great deal of what we might want to say about the observable world could be analyzed through the logical apparatus he laid out in the book, to be built up systematically from the most simple and elementary propositions. And, as he insisted, although our language worked properly on the surface, underlying that surface were quite different elements and structures: "Language disguises thought.... The tacit conventions on which the understanding of everyday language depends are enormously complicated.... The apparent logical form of a proposition need not be its real one."[3] Thus we are able to speak meaningfully without having any idea how a word or a proposition has sense. That will be revealed only in pursuing the logical analysis that Wittgenstein, following Russell and the much admired logician Frege, was undertaking. Analyzing language through logic in this way would show that the way in which language actually worked was quite different from how it might look on the surface. More than that, it would also resolve many troubling problems, such as wondering how propositions apparently referring to objects that did not exist could actually make sense if they referred to nothing (and remember that Wittgenstein held that the most basic names had to refer to existing objects). If they referred to nonexistent objects, then nonexistent objects must exist, which seems contradictory; but if they referred to nothing, how could they have meaning? Would not all names for nonexistent objects have the same meaning? All talk about objects that did not exist would actually have the same reference, not the nonexistent king of France, or a nonexistent unicorn, but in both cases referring to the same thing, just *nothing*? This was just one of the many problems that seemed to dissolve under the new logic that Wittgenstein, following Russell and Frege, was developing in the *Tractatus*.

For our purposes here we need go no further into any of this, beyond emphasizing that, according to Wittgenstein's so-called picture theory, true propositions were those that were identical in form to some actually existing fact or state of affairs, or to complexes of such. It was this rooting of elementary propositions in basic simple facts that gave language its validity and sense. Unfortunately, though, we could and often did use language to talk about things that could not be reduced to these elementary facts, and so went far beyond anything we would be entitled to say. Anyone

---

3. Wittgenstein, *Tractatus Logico-Philosophicus*, 37 (props 4.002–21).

who "wanted to say something metaphysical"—something that is, that was not rooted firmly in basic facts but was engaging in airy speculation—would have failed to give a meaning to his words.[4] And this was because there would be no picturable fact or collection of facts to which such talk could align or correspond. In particular, talk of values, of ethics, aesthetics, and religion, would all be attempts to go beyond what could meaningfully be said. Language would fail to denote the purported objects apparently being referred to, because there were no such objects, or it would fail to capture what was being said of them, or both. They would be meaningless, in other words.

Wittgenstein's *Tractatus*, with its rigid distinction between meaningful and meaningless discourse (i.e., scientific talk, as opposed to supposedly value-laden pseudo-talk), became highly influential after it was published in 1921. It may be that no one really understood what it was saying, not least because of difficulties in knowing just what the elementary propositions were supposed to be. Notwithstanding its obscurity, however, it was certainly taken by the most avant-garde philosophers of the time (mainly logicians in Vienna, Warsaw, and Berlin) to be showing, or at least asserting, the primacy of scientific discourse and the failure of non-scientific talk, or at least of non-observational talk, to make sense. The *Tractatus* became iconic for cutting-edge philosophy in the 1920s and 1930s; according to Moritz Schlick, the key figure in Viennese philosophy at the time, the *Tractatus* was a decisive turning point for him and his colleagues. Wittgenstein himself was originally from Vienna, where his work was earnestly studied in the 1920s and 1930s, while he himself was either teaching in primary schools in lower Austria or establishing himself as a major figure in the Cambridge philosophical faculty (and later throughout the English-speaking world).

Its dismissal of metaphysical talk as meaningless became foundational among the so-called logical positivists of the philosophical Vienna Circle of the 1930s and continued in different forms to influence their followers in Britain and the USA, such

---

4. Wittgenstein, *Tractatus Logico-Philosophicus*, 151 (prop 6.53).

as W. V. O. Quine and Nelson Goodman in Harvard and A. J. Ayer in Oxford. For the logician Quine, talk of existence itself is eviscerated of any significance. To say that something is (or exists) is no more than a means of pointing out that some property can be found in the world. In his deathless (and much quoted) formula, "to be is to be the value of a variable"—in other words, saying that something (e.g., my dog) exists is reduced to asserting that a certain property or description (in this case O'Hear's dog) can legitimately feature in a sentence I might be disposed to utter.[5] Nothing follows or can be inferred from that about the worth or value or meaning of this particular creature's life or existence. All is flattened out into a mere description having application, with no question of the meaning or value of any particular existent.

And what leads me to use that or any other description? The answer was supplied to me by Ayer himself, who, years later, told me that the book one should study was Goodman's *The Structure of Appearance*. This classic work was published in 1951 but was based on work done far earlier. In it Goodman's aim was show that our whole worldview of solid objects, properties, scientific theories, and so on should be seen as being constructed from the momentary and simple sensory states or sense data of individual perceivers. So the descriptions one was disposed to use—about that dog, this house, her friends, my children, and so on—were themselves constructed out of the momentary sense impression or data that hit the speaker's retinal and other sensory surfaces at one time or another. Though in *The Tractatus* Wittgenstein never talked about sense data, the things Goodman was taking as fundamental, Goodman's reductive methodology, which built up what we normally say and think from utterly simple sensory foundations, was not altogether unlike Wittgenstein's picture of basic facts and the elementary propositions that referred to them.

According to logical positivism, as trenchantly expounded by Ayer in his iconoclastic *Language Truth and Logic* of 1936, only statements based either on logic or verifiable observation were meaningful. Otherwise, they were meaningless. Flaws were

---

5. Quine, "On What There Is," 15.

quickly discovered in this so-called "verification principle." The verification principle itself it was neither a matter of pure logic nor verifiable in experience, so, by its own rule, it rendered itself meaningless. Nor were the theories of science, which the principle was invoked to prioritize above all other forms of talk, themselves verifiable; being universal in scope, covering all space and time and so going way beyond what we or any of us could verify, they could not themselves be verified, and so they too would be meaningless on the principle.

No matter, if the strict verification principle could not be sustained, its spirit, in some modified form, continued and continues to dominate in much current philosophy and beyond (especially among self-declared "public intellectuals" of the Russell stripe). Science is the touchstone of reality and attempts to talk about things beyond the scientifically accessible are illusory, delusory, irrational, dishonest, childish, merely expressions of emotion, in a word, unserious, morally disreputable, unworthy of intelligent scrutiny or attention.

Wittgenstein's *Tractatus* may have foreshadowed or even instigated much of what is now taken as serious thinking on matters of value and religion. But even while he was formulating the positions in the *Tractatus*, which his philosophical odyssey led him later to reject, his was very far from the scientistic spirit of those who took their lead from it. He was always a far more complex, even tortured, soul. He was definitely a soul. He was never dismissive of the religious spirit. In his *Notebooks 1914–1916*, from the time he was developing the ideas in the *Tractatus*, he tantalizingly wrote: "To believe in a God means that the facts of the world are not the end of the matter."[6] He is talking here of the facts as delivered by modern science, those to which in the *Tractatus* he wished to confine the sayable, and to which many of those who followed in his footsteps wished to confine the intelligible. But for Wittgenstein, and whatever he might have believed about "a God," the facts of the world were never the end of the matter.

---

6. Wittgenstein, *Notebooks 1914–1916*, 74.

Not the End of the Matter

Whatever he might have proposed in the *Tractatus* about sayability, his own view was always far more nuanced: in the preface to the *Tractatus* itself, he famously wrote, "How little is achieved when these problems are solved."[7] He was referring here to those problems of philosophy with which he had concerned himself in his early work, and dare I say, also the problems of natural science. Wittgenstein's friend Paul Engelmann commented that in delimiting the sayable in the *Tractatus* Wittgenstein had sought to describe "not the coastline of that island which he is bent on surveying with such meticulous accuracy, but the boundary of the ocean."[8] We are a world away from Russell and the logical positivists who closed their eyes to the ocean beyond the shore on which they were stranded, and embraced Wittgenstein's thought with such misunderstanding.

Wittgenstein's later thought, particularly as expounded in the posthumous *Philosophical Investigations* of 1953, can be seen as a repudiation of the *Tractatus*'s view of language. There is no single simple logical form to which meaningful speech must conform, nor is there any deep structure beneath the surface. We have no need to dig for supposedly necessary conditions for the possibility of language. Language is a crucial aspect of our lives, all our lives, and it works just as it is, embedded in the practices we all engage in. There is no need to look for anything beneath the surface of our language or experience. To think that there is, as Wittgenstein himself did in his earlier thinking, would be to commit a philosophical fallacy. Just look, carefully, at how language actually works, at how we naturally act and react. To paraphrase two later Wittgensteinian aphorisms: there is nothing hidden here. And: don't think, look.[9]

There are many forms of language, all of which have their uses in our lives. Indeed, it is in being used in our lives in multifarious ways that language has its life and meaning. There are many

7. Wittgenstein, *Tractatus Logico-Philosophicus*, 5.

8. Engelmann, *Letters from Ludwig Wittgenstein*, 97.

9. See Wittgenstein, *Philosophical Investigations*, 128 (section 435) and 31 (section 66).

different types of language, "language games" Wittgenstein called them, with their own purposes and structures. To find out how any particular language game worked, we need to look at the use it plays in the lives of the people who were using it. What had been condemned in the *Tractatus* as meaningless was not meaningless. Even religious talk was meaningful in its context, though misunderstandings here and elsewhere would arise if people attempt to theorize about what is meant in ways that distort the original linguistic practice in which the talk has its home.

On religious language, while not being formally religious himself, Wittgenstein argued strongly that misunderstandings arose when critics of religion, like the anthropologist Sir James Frazer, try to interpret what is going on in a religious ritual as a primitive attempt to manipulate events in the world. They are thus misguidedly seeing religion as a type of technology or science. Wittgenstein wrote that "it is nonsense to say that the characteristic feature of these [i.e., ritualistic] actions is that they spring from wrong ideas about the physics of things. (This is what Frazer does when he says that magic is really false physics, or as the case may be, false medicine, technology, etc.)."[10] Frazer's monumental and influential *Golden Bough* (completed in 1915) was Wittgenstein's target here, but one can predict what he would have said of a so-called new atheist of our day treating the God of religious practice as if he were a powerful but somewhat incompetent or even malicious super-human agent.

In a note from 1946, late in his life, Wittgenstein said that "it strikes me that a religious belief could only be something like a passionate commitment to a system of reference. Hence, although it's a *belief*, it's really a way of living, a way of assessing life. It's passionately seizing hold of *this* interpretation."[11] We will have much more to say later about the way that a religious myth can be seen as an assessment or an interpretation of life, and about how, as such, it will differ from a scientific description of explanation. Religious, including mythical, talk and scientific discourse are different

---

10. Wittgenstein, "Remarks on Frazer's *Golden Bough*," 33.
11. Wittgenstein, *Culture and Value*, 64.

language games with their own focus, function, and legitimacy, and the one should not be seen as invalidating the other. Without developing this point further here, at the moment we will simply note the way in which Wittgenstein, early as well as late, never thought that a scientific account of the world could close off our understanding of it. And this remains true even if in his early work, like the logical positivists, and before he developed his conception of language games and the diversity of linguistic forms and uses, he thought that nothing could be said beyond what science told us.

In pointing to the limitations of scientific discourse, Wittgenstein was not intending to disparage the importance of science or of logical analysis, let alone their truth, nor indeed am I. No one whose mind is not obstinately closed to human achievement can fail to be mightily impressed by the successes and discoveries, theoretical and practical, of science since the seventeenth century. But in this area we would do well to ponder the wise words of Peter Hacker: "Every source of truth is unavoidably a source of falsehood, from which its own canons of reasoning and confirmation attempt to protect it. But it can also become a source of conceptual confusion, and consequently of intellectual myth-making. . . . It is the task of philosophy to defend us against such illusions of reason."[12] It may at first sight be hard to see contemporary natural science as a source of intellectual mythmaking, as I am sure Hacker intended we should. However, as we shall see, there is an important sense in which science itself is a source of intellectual mythmaking.

We in the twenty-first century are highly attuned to the idea that science, with all its success and prestige, indeed because of its success and prestige, is itself the touchstone of reality. Even the predictions of climate catastrophe, which have led many to a hostile attitude to scientific development and technological improvement, are actually couched in scientific terms, and are expounded as relying for their truth on "the" science from which they derive their credibility.

12. Hacker, "Wittgenstein and the Autonomy of Humanistic Understanding," 73.

But, quite apart from the myths within science—such as that the brain is the mind, that machines can think, that quantum theory forces us to contemplate the reality of multiverses, that we are prisoners of our genes, or that all phenomena are reducible to the atomic and subatomic theories of physics—the conviction that science is itself the touchstone of reality is itself a myth in no way justified by what the theories of science actually tell us. After all, the very idea that science is the touchstone of reality, is not itself to be found in any scientific theory and could not be verified scientifically. Further, the theories of science we accept are in the end found acceptable only because they are tested against our non-scientific, everyday experience and truth-seeking, from which they emerge. So, for the theories science to be seen as undermining or downplaying our everyday experience with its nose for truth is to put them at risk of losing their own credibility. Science itself emerges from the work and investigations of human beings, with the very capacities and freedoms that some hardline scientists and philosophers would downplay as mere dispensable *façons de parler* or dismiss altogether as illusions. Such hardliners leave the very theories from which they derive their skepticism about human freedom and rationality hanging in the air, deprived of the essential context from which they emerge, and where they find their support in observations made by free, rational human beings. But where I would finesse what Hacker is saying is in the suggestion, which I am about to defend in this book, that there is in human life a positive role for myth and even mythmaking (mythopoeia), if not for all myths or any myth making.

"To believe in God means to see that life has a meaning, . . . that we *are* in a certain sense dependent, and that what we are dependent on we can call God." So continues the passage from the *Notebooks* to which we have already referred.[13] But, as readers of Wittgenstein, early and late, will be aware, Wittgenstein was highly fastidious in this area, still in his later years characterizing much talk about value as mere chatter. Even more, he remained highly

---

13. Wittgenstein, *Notebooks*, 74.

reluctant to *say* anything about God. And so should we be, so long as we remain on the purely descriptive level.

Our reasoning powers cannot escape the stifling embrace of the so-called Kantian antinomies. In his *Critique of Pure Reason* of 1781, Kant listed a number of crucial areas where whatever we might want positively to assert, the contrary can also and with equal reason be affirmed.[14] Kant called these apparent dilemmas "the antinomies of pure reason," and they arise particularly where we want to assert things about the cosmos or universe as a whole. In Kant's view, the problems stem from illegitimate attempts on our part to apply notions like cause and time, which make sense *within* the world, to the world *as a whole*, something that is all but inevitable when we start talking about a God or a creator beyond or outside the universe. The antinomies that are particularly relevant to talk about God are whether or not the world has a beginning in time and limits in space, and whether the world has a cause that is it itself necessary. If the world is limited, as orthodox talk of a creator might well imply, does this mean that it emerged from nothing? But how can something come from nothing? If the world has a cause outside itself, that cause must at some point begin to act so as to produce the world, so it would not be outside the world and would itself belong to the world. We could add to Kant's argument here that if the world needs a cause that is outside the world, would that supposed "necessary" cause not itself need a cause, and so on through any system of causes. And if space is limited or bounded, what lies outside the bounds of space? On the other hand, just how are we to think of it going on endlessly? From Kant's point of view, the problems arise in this area from treating or attempting to treat the world as a whole as if it were itself an object within the world, illegitimately to apply to the world as a whole concepts—such as cause, temporal beginning, and spatial limit—which have their place only within the world.

Well before Kant, and more generally, theologians from Aquinas on have always warned us that in attempting to describe the divine we have to use terms derived from ordinary language,

---

14. See Kant, *Critique of Pure Reason*, 396–402 and 415–21.

but in an *analogical* way—that is to say, in an extended non-literal sense. As Aquinas puts it, "we cannot grasp what God is, but only what He is not, and how other things are related to Him." Further, while God is one and simple, unlike things on earth, "our intellect knows Him [i.e., God] according to diverse conceptions because it cannot see Him as He is in Himself."[15] Ralph McInerny, the well-known Thomist philosopher, says that Aquinas insists that "God reveals himself to us through images and likenesses. Scripture is figurative and metaphorical, which is a concession to what is easily grasped by the human mind."[16] This has radical implications, which we will explore further as we go on. For the moment we can simply note that if Christian scripture is figurative and metaphorical, it can neither be the whole truth about God, nor is it necessarily in conflict with other figurative and metaphorical accounts of God or the divine, any more than a poem by Coleridge is necessarily in conflict with one by Byron: *Kubla Khan* is not contradicted by *Don Juan*—both may intimate truths about the human condition, though from very different perspectives. And so, I will suggest, it may be with religious myths from different traditions.

Kant himself, like Aquinas, and unlike modern atheists or agnostics, did want to preserve the possibility of talking or at least of thinking about God. In order to do this, he developed a notion of what he called the noumenal, that is a realm in which there was a reality that was beyond or behind the ordinarily knowable world of experience. He saw God and talk of God, and indeed talk of morality, as belonging to the noumenal, that is as underlying our experience, but in such a way as to be undescribable if we attempted to use the language of science and ordinary factuality. He hoped thus to avoid the antinomies and other difficulties arising from attempts to speak about God or indeed about human freedom, which itself can seem problematic when we start thinking about the causes of our actions. (If our free actions are caused by psychological and genetic factors, they are not free; but if they are

---

15. Aquinas, *Summa Contra Gentiles*, 1.30.4; Aquinas, *Summa Theologica*, 1.13.12.

16. McInery, ed., *Thomas Aquinas, Selected Writings*, xx.

not so caused, are they random and inexplicable, coming from nowhere?)

What both Kant and Aquinas are pointing to here are the difficulties that necessarily arise when we attempt to use concepts that have their use in descriptions and explanations of the empirical world, and within the empirical world, outside that use. This could be seen as part of what Hacker is warning us against in his talk of a source of truth becoming a source of falsehood, a source of intellectual mythmaking. But, as Aquinas, rather than Kant, insists, for those religiously inclined, at least, the attempt has to be made.

As Wittgenstein says, we can see life as having a meaning, and doing so will inevitably engender talk and thought about God. Is there a way of going beyond Wittgenstein's own initial self-denying ordinance of remaining silent where one cannot legitimately speak? One can perfectly well accept the point of the Kantian antinomies if they are seen as applying to what can be stated and examined within the terms of natural science, to what Wittgenstein referred to as the totality of facts that constitute the world. And they will also limit what can meaningfully be said about the world as a whole.[17] After all, as Kant himself was insistent, in a scientific description or explanation, notions of value, moral or aesthetic, will not feature, except in the rare occasions in which such things are the items to be explained. The same goes for our human emotions and institutions more generally, which is why when we start to look at our activity in terms of scientific explanations talk of human freedom and indeed of morality begins to seem problematic. Freedom is hard if not impossible to reconcile with scientific accounts of the way the world works, while notions of moral value find no place in such accounts. It is for this reason that Kant introduced his notion of the noumenal, as a realm beyond the factual and imperceptible to ordinary sight, but which somehow impinges on us, in which we see ourselves as free. It is also subject to the absolute and unconditional demands of a moral sense of which

---

17. See Wittgenstein, *Tractatus Logico-Philosophicus*, 7 (props 1.1–12) and 151 (prop 6.53).

we are all aware, but that find no place in the realm of scientific understanding.

Maybe we do not need to resort to so drastic a move, a move that has puzzled and entranced Kant's admirers ever since he formulated the notion; in thinking of our human life and activity it is enough to say that we live in a way in which notions of freedom, responsibility, and value are central and indispensable, and as already observed, it is from human life as conceived and lived in such terms that science itself emerges. So quasi-scientific talk about the causes of our behavior cannot undermine our freedom or other concepts central to what we are thinking of as the *Lebenswelt*, the world in which we live and move and have our being. To put this point in another way, we could say that in our everyday talk about human life, with notions like freedom, responsibility, love, betrayal, gratitude, and so on, we are employing a different language game from that of science, which finds no place for such things in its causal accounts of the physical world. Science is what it is as an account of the world that abstracts from the motley of experience only those aspects of the world that can be captured in its value-free generalizations.

Natural science aims to explain the data it is examining in observer-independent terms; as such, terms peculiar to the human *Lebenswelt* will not feature in them, which is why scientific investigations into human behavior will never displace our understanding of ourselves in human terms. Scientific explanations do not operate on that level, and this will be true even if the scientific enquiry in question is about human life and has its point and motivation in our aims and desires. Thus, for example, a scientific investigation of a disease, such as cancer, is about our bodily existence and will doubtless be driven by human aims and desires. But its validity will depend on its being couched and verified in terms that are objective and independent of the feelings of the investigators. Equally, we, as human beings as well as scientists, may decide not to pursue research into some highly volatile and dangerous pathogen, but this will say nothing about whatever truth might lie there, awaiting discovery, so to speak, which our science might reveal if it got the chance. That is independent of our choices in the area. It may well be partly because of this independence of the results from what we think or wish that scientists are less inhibited in what they research into than perhaps they should be. (Some of those who developed the atom bomb later came to feel that they should have been more inhibited in their research, and, more recently, some of us might also feel about the hubristic attempt of Chinese and American scientists to develop Covid viruses, under the utilitarian doctrine of "gain of function," presumably meaning that such potentially dangerous things should be investigated to see what benefits might thereby accrue.)

To sum up, what has been shown in this chapter is the sense in which the constraints of science and the *Tractatus* are, in Wittgenstein's words, "not the end of the matter." What we now need to do is to examine how in our thought and behavior we are able to transcend those constraints. As we will see, a key way of opening our lives to wider and more generous perspectives is by means of the myths that have captivated humanity in pretty well all the societies of which we have knowledge. In engaging with myth we will, of course, be breaking the bounds of what, according to the positivists, can be said, but, as Wittgenstein himself came to realize, to restrict our universe to what is scientifically expressible is itself artificial and inhuman.

2

The Place of Myth in Human Life

IN THE EMPIRICAL WORLD as envisaged by Kant and the early Wittgenstein, so long as we are sticking to what is scientifically admissible, everything pertaining to human subjectivity becomes only a datum to be explained scientifically. This is because the aim of science is precisely to describe and explain the world and its contents, including ourselves, in a way that is completely objective and neutral as between possible observers. The aim of science to yield an account of the world in entirely general terms, abstracting from the perspectives and sensibility of particular observers. To use the paradoxical phrase of Thomas Nagel, what is attempted in science is "a view from nowhere," an account of the world that would be available to *any* observer, human, nonhuman, or even extraterrestrial, and whatever their position, sensory make-up, or feelings about the world. In the world as described in modern science, the *Lebenswelt*, the world in which we live, is effectively by-passed. Talk about our feelings, our values, our intentions, our perceptions, our activity, our institutions, our sense of obligation and duty, our sense of awe and gratitude, and that certain facets of our lives, and our lives themselves, are to be treated as sacred and inherently valuable—all these key aspects of our actual existence, and much more, are either sidelined in scientific enquiry, as merely epiphenomenal effects of the more robust particles of physics, or dismissed altogether. But only in scientific enquiry.

As we will show in more detail later, the mystery of existence and of the nature of our world is not explained away by science so much as revealed and is, in its way, demanding an explanation of an altogether different sort. How is it that the natural processes that lead to the wonders we experience on earth, both organic and inorganic, came about? How is it that they were, so to speak, foreshadowed from the start of the universe—if there were such a thing—and are still sustained billions of years later? We will need some account of why the laws and processes described in science are as they are, and specifically how it is that they were and are such as to yield life and consciousness, and our own pondering on such things.

Neither can the value-laden aspects of our human life be dismissed or explained away even by the most recondite and mind-boggling theories of modern science. Just because we are creatures of flesh and blood and of all the processes that underpin our flesh and blood in no way invalidates or contradicts the experience we have as persons, replete with notions of truth, goodness (and its opposite), and beauty. One way of seeing this is to consider how the experience of each one of us is structured, and to see why this initial structuring of our experience cannot be displaced either by science or by philosophical reflection.

To begin with philosophy, philosophers in the empiricist tradition of David Hume and his more recent followers, such as Ayer and Goodman, hold that all our knowledge and thinking begins from sensory data private to each one of us. On this view, these momentary experiences are the only things of which we can be absolutely certain; they are prior to all our other beliefs and thoughts. Then from these momentary experiences we build up a picture of the world as going beyond what is in the experience of each individual perceiver, as consisting of objects and people and realities with an existence independent of our elementary experiences.

This empiricist conception of knowledge and experience, which dominated Anglo-American philosophical thinking for some large part of the twentieth century and even beyond, has a convergence with scientific accounts of our experience. On these accounts our experience of the world arises from sensory inputs from a world quite different from how we think of it. These inputs are then transformed by our brains scrambling them to give us the commonsense view basic to the world in which we live and move and have our being, the *Lebenswelt*, as, following Husserl, the world of our experience has come to be known. Then, as a further part of our transforming of the sensory inputs we receive from the mysterious but value-free world of subatomic particles and the rest, we will graft on notions of value, of right and wrong, as produced by our feelings and reactions to the pleasure and pain we experience in being stimulated by the sensory inputs we are conscious of. In Hume's telling phrase, our seeing value and beauty and even disvalue and ugliness in the world is a matter of our "gilding and staining" a value-free worldly canvas in which there are really no moral or aesthetic qualities. We will also build up a sense that there are other agents like ourselves, whom we will picture as being free and responsible, subject to judgments of guilt, shame, honor, virtue, courage, and the rest.

But to some adherents of the scientific account, and indeed of philosophical empiricism, all this will be seen as a form of make-believe, a human construction imposed on a world in which no such things are really to be found. Strictly speaking, it will be said, we live in a value-free world of elementary particles and the rest or of momentary sensory inputs, which are the true causes of what we are and what we do. Everything over and above these elementary particles and inputs is constructed by our minds or brains as a practically useful but ultimately misleading way of making our way through the buzzing, booming penumbra of experience hitting our sense organs at any moment.

But pictures of this sort, whether expressed in terms of philosophical empiricism or of rigorous scientific theorizing, badly misrepresent the nature of human experience and indeed of the world. From the very start, our *experience* is not of our sense organs being stimulated by microscopic particles or forces, but of our being in a world of objects and people that are influencing us, interacting with us, corroborating some of what we do and think and correcting other aspects of our personal perspectives. Even our current experience at any moment does not consist of momentary or instant sensory points, as the accounts we are questioning would have it. All our experience contains within it a reference to the past through the memory built into any present experience and also an openness to the future we are already moving into.

If we watch the development of a baby, we can see how the baby as it were wakes up into the world in which it is living by responding to the people around it, to the objects it is surrounded by, to the noises it hears, and to the feelings lavished on it. The baby is not cut off from that world, having to reach out to the world through interpreting sensory signals from a realm beyond its experience. In looking at how the baby develops, there is no sense that it is delving into its own mind or brain and somehow constructing objects or building up a world from photons hitting its retina. It is not cut off from that world, but it is immediately in the world as we perceive it. It begins to be aware of that world, and then to move around in it, learning at the same time how to deal with its environment and the people in its ambience, learning too to use and enjoy the language its parents and others speak. Our most primitive experience is of the world as it is, as it appears to us, prior to scientific or philosophical theorizing. The world as it is and as it presents itself to us will include a network of values which are an integral part of the life into which we all emerge from birth.

I have expressed what I am wanting to say here in terms of the way babies begin to live in the human world, because this can give us a helpful picture of how things are. But the same result will emerge if, as adults, we each ask ourselves without introducing any philosophical or scientific theorizing what our experience is like, what it consists in. The answer will not be that we are constructing a picture of the world and its enduring solid objects from momentary sensory data we passively receive and which we then build into what we all know from common sense. It will be that we are already fully and immediately active in the world, which is a world of objects, people, values, and so on, and that we know about this world immediately through the way it acts on us and we on it. We can, of course, go on to analyze our sensory experience of the world in which we live in terms of philosophical speculation (sense data and so on) or of scientific accounts of sensory experience (photons, retinas, brain activity). But this will only be by means of prizing off a part of our experience from the whole in which it has its existence. Contrary to Hume's account, all such analyses will of necessity be secondary to our primitive experience of the world, stemming from this basic experience and reliant upon it. We would be in error if, like Hume, we thought that these secondary analyses could somehow discredit or undermine that primitive experience from which they come and on which their plausibility rests. For we can only judge these secondary accounts by seeing how far they are corroborated or not in terms of our basic experience of the world. We have nothing else on which to test our theories about our experience, or indeed about anything else, be they philosophical or scientific.

Our lives thus transcend science and scientific explanation, even where such explanations impinge partially on our self-understanding. Such explanations, of necessity abstracting from important dimensions of our experience, can never be complete or reduce completely how we are in the *Lebenswelt*. Our deeply rooted sense of freedom, both our own and that of others, and our sense in our dealings with each other that we are dealing with persons, replete with their own often surprising reactions and choices, all go beyond the mechanistic, biological, and psychological accounts of our activity offered in the sciences of human behavior. These secondary accounts can give us only partial and at times skewed pictures of the actual human beings we encounter in our lives. And they are accepted or not by the way they produce results observable and checkable against the realities of the primitive experiential picture of the world from which the theorizing emerges, against the structure of the *Lebenswelt*, in other words.

Essential to our existence on the level of the *Lebenswelt*, we are self-conscious seekers of meaning. As such, naturally and inevitably we want to explore the reasons for our existence, where, in a meaningful sense, we came from, where we are going, and ultimately the being or beings to whom we owe our existence. Nowadays, as intellectual heirs to post-Kantian and post-Enlightenment thinking, we may feel that these questions have no answers and are unanswerable, but this is a recent development in human history. For most of human history, and still predominantly the case today, the vast majority of humans have found these questions of ultimate significance and have answered them not in quasi-scientific terms, but in terms of what I will call myths, those endlessly fascinating poetic and dramatic expressions of hidden truths, to adapt a description of myth by the poet D. M. Thomas, himself a weaver of mythical fiction. Or, in the words of Ted Hughes, reflecting on the way particular myths have become embedded and developed in the life of a people or community, so that after a while just one or two words from the myth will serve to remind the hearer of its whole canvas: "They not only attract and light up everything relevant in our own experience; they are also in continual private meditation, . . . they are little factories of understanding. New revelations of meaning open out of their images and patterns continually, stirred into reach by our own growth and changing circumstances."[1]

As will become clear, while truths can be embedded in myths of all types, what I will be concentrating on in this essay will be myths that have become central to a culture or, even more, to a religion. These will often be myths that have long historical roots. Indeed, in some cases their origins may be lost in prehistory, in the distant past. Even when, as with Christianity or Islam, one can point to a moment in history when a myth might be said to have begun, from its point of origin the myth will have undergone a long development and evolution in the community that is itself formed by it. Indeed, in both these cases, the "new" myth has its roots deep in an earlier and less historically determinate myth, in these cases the ancient Hebraic tradition. What the ancient roots and the steady evolutionary development of a myth conspire to

---

1. Hughes, "Myth and Education."

show is the way the myth forms the community it belongs to and conforms to its needs and insights.

    I do not want to say that myths that do not have a long and or religious provenance may not also have features in common with those that do, and I will say a little about that later. But one of the things that interests me about myths is the way that some of them—the ones I am primarily interested in—form a kind of matrix in which belief, commitment, and community are imperceptibly linked. Though they do or have involved belief, typically they also structure or have structured moral and other attitudes, and often membership of a community as well. Some are, in a sense, "dead" myths, in that there is no longer a community that embraces them as living sources of inspiration and attitude. This would be the case nowadays with the ancient Greek or Norse myths, for example; but, as we see with many thinkers and poets of more recent times, they may still carry a charge that continues to move and fascinate, even indeed to shape behavior and morality. In myths we are typically presented with a view of human life that goes way beyond the biological and scientific imperatives to survive and reproduce, to avoid pain and seek pleasure. To take an example, even the most apparently self-seeking and heartless of heroes, Achilles in *The Iliad* perhaps, is shown to prefer honor and death to a long life and, in the last resort, is overcome with compassion and fellow-feeling toward his sworn enemy. Not all mythical heroes are as admirable as Achilles, nor do all myths present so sympathetic a moral, but in general they all present us with a much richer and many-textured picture of life than the scientific account, and in doing so will influence their listeners in their own behavior. Similarly, as I will also argue later, those brought up to follow one myth, Christianity for example, may come to derive inspiration and consolation from the myths of other peoples, treating them not as mere fictions, but as something more potent and revelatory.

    One key feature of the religious and culture-forming myths I am interested in here is that they picture us humans, we seekers of meaning, as part of an order of value that is beyond the purely empirical or scientific, and, crucially, an order that we do not create. What these myths present is an order to which we are subject, which is why, so often, the myth itself delves deep into prehistory, in the manner of a creation story. A myth may have its own roots in traditions and customs whose history is no longer visible or accessible to us, traditions that may themselves be prehistoric. To the extent that we engage with a value-conferring religious or cultural myth, even if we see its surface content and structure as metaphorical or allegorical, as not literally true, we will be moved to take its underlying message to be of and from an order we do not create. Its message represents a cosmic reality that is not a mere projection or human construction but something that founds our sense of value and meaning, something by which we are bound. For those attracted to or moved by such a myth, it must be much more than a projection; it must be reaching out to or from a reality beyond the world as revealed in everyday life and science. Even though inevitably filtered through human thought and expression, it will be regarded, with some reason I will argue, as a revelation from beyond the world in which we live. It will be showing the meaning there is for us humans in a world that on its face is indifferent to us and our concerns. That such myths, treated in this way, are ubiquitous throughout human history and culture is surely significant, and should also lead us to question the claim of any scientific accounts of the world telling us that they alone are complete and exhaustive as descriptions of reality. The prevalence of such myths clearly points to something deep in human nature, and the scientific criticisms of some aspects of mythical accounts of the world and its origin cannot diminish the fundamental mystery of existence and of the origin or source of the universe. For some, indeed, the scientific accounts will only serve to deepen the wonder.

More fundamentally, the prevalence of such myths should lead us to be skeptical of accounts of mythology in purely functional or utilitarian terms. The guiding myth of a culture or a religion certainly does have a social function, and is useful in many mundane worldly or social ways. It can correctly be seen as part of what binds a community together, in giving a people ceremonies, rituals, and modes of conduct to structure their lives individually and collectively. But that does not show why the community in question is so bound, why a myth so convinces the people to bind themselves by its means. Its followers adhere to the myth because of what it shows and says, not because of what it does. They see the world as structured in its terms. Nor does it show why, contra Frazer in *The Golden Bough*, myths that ostensibly involve the manipulation of nature outlive refutations of their predictive claims. They continue to hold a people when the predictions and manipulations manifestly fail to work, and even when the community in question has ceased to focus on the myth's predictions (as perhaps when the early Christians ceased to expect an imminent second coming of Christ). The implication is that in the myths we are thinking about there is a transcendent core that holds the people and inspires them to look for sacred bonds beyond the technological, the predictive, and the sociological. The myths we are primarily considering characteristically import transcendent destinies and obligations. They disclose aspects of the world beyond its apparent indifference and meaninglessness. To the ultimately helpless individual we all are from the worldly point of view, facing struggle, pain, and ultimately death, they articulate connections to the divine or divinities, on a different level from any worldly benefits. In typically presenting this world as one of struggle and exile, they allow the individual to see a value in the struggle and suffering all have to undergo, to disclose them as something other than just parts of the mechanism of a blind and indifferent universe.[2]

I need to stress once more that in calling something a myth I am not implying that it is untrue. As I will argue shortly, a myth may well be true, in the sense of being based on actual historical facts, but its truth is not that of a purely factual historical or scientific account. Myths may have a factual, empirical basis, but in a myth any empirical facts on which it is based will be given a meaning well beyond the empirical. Thus, to take an utterly familiar example, to us in the West and in the Christian world more widely

---

2. I have drawn in the last three paragraphs on Kolakowski, *The Meaning of Myth*.

The Place of Myth in Human Life

the most familiar of all: a charismatic Jewish preacher was born in Judaea in the time of the Roman emperor Augustus. He was put to death in Jerusalem around AD 33, after which his followers preached his resurrection, and gained many converts. These are historical, empirical facts, recognized by contemporary writers such as Josephus, and no doubt by many others subsequently with no investment in the matter, but who look at the historical record in an impartial, objective way. That this preacher was the Son of God, the incarnated second "person" of the Blessed Trinity, and that his death brought about the redemption of the whole world—these meanings are what I am calling mythical. In similar vein, Muhammad is a verifiably historical figure, born in Mecca around AD 570, who went on to found a new religion in the Arabian world. That he was the divinely inspired prophet of Islam, the last prophet indeed, with a vital revelation for the whole of humankind, goes beyond the pure and verifiable historical facts. To the believer in Christ or in Muhammad the mythical interpretations of the historical facts are as true as the facts they interpret, but they are apparent only to those with the eyes of faith.

We human beings are not like animals, living completely submerged in the present. We are self-conscious, able to stand outside the present moment and experience. As already noted a few paragraphs ago, we relate the moment we are in to the past and to the possibilities of the future. We try to make sense of our lives from this reflective, ecstatic viewpoint. As we stand apart from what we are and what is the case at the present moment, we survey our situation from either a short-term or a long-term perspective. We try to make sense of our lives, and to do this we have to go beyond the historical, social, biological, and physical facts on which we can all agree, and that are supported by empirical evidence. We have to endow these facts with *meaning*. We have to find meaning in them and beyond.

Our lives are not lived as a series of meaningless moments, but are interpreted against the background of a trans-temporal story. *Chronos*, moment-after-moment time, one damn thing after another, becomes *kairos*, a time in which particular events in our lives take on a crucial significance within an extended narrative, one crucially we see as handed down to us, rather than as one we create.

As self-conscious and reflective beings we are impelled to go beyond satisfying the purely biological imperatives for food, shelter, and sex. In order to do this, from time immemorial, all human cultures that we know of have had recourse to myths. Myths are stories or narratives that encapsulate what our feelings and attitudes are and should be. Myths place these reflections against a canvas that often includes super-human and super-terrestrial beings, such as gods and spirits, as well as ancestors and kings, and legendary heroes and villains. Even while remaining on a purely anthropological plane, and suspending judgment about the reality of the events and beings encapsulated in these myths, it can be seen that within them the myths often contain truths of a human sort, truths suffused with value. These are truths about the right way to live, about virtue and vice, about heroism and cowardice, about how to face death and life, about one's duties to one's ancestors and to one's descendants, as well as the attitudes appropriate to all kinds of everyday situations in which we find ourselves. In talking of myth in what follows I will mostly be referring to mythical narratives that tell of the origins of the world, of God and gods, and of the dealings of humans and gods. Central to what I am talking of will be those myths that have been vital to the life and culture of peoples from time immemorial, including, of course, those of the great world religions.

Religious myths of the sort I am referring to here and later in this essay will have found widespread acceptance within a community, and, as we have seen, their sources or origins may well be lost in the mists of distant time. Even in the case of myths, such as Christianity or Islam, that have definite origins in recorded history, they will encompass and draw on long-past events, often supposed to be beyond recorded or remembered history, or even dating to the very beginning of the world. They will characteristically put reliance on histories or memories earlier than the events or occurrences with which they themselves deal directly. Because of their communal acceptance and their multifaceted longevity, in their form and attraction they will manifest a type of objectivity or a penumbra of age that would not attach to a myth we see as created by an identifiable historical individual, even if that individual were a Richard Wagner or a J. R. R. Tolkien (though it is not coincidental that in their powerful mythmaking both Wagner and Tolkien were actually drawing substantially on ancient and venerable myths).

In this objectivity and timeless historicity the myths I am focusing on will raise their individual adherents out of their self-centeredness and solitude into something beyond. In immersing him- or herself in a myth, the individual will feel part of a community with widely shared and unquestioned values, and in most cases, a community that sees itself as rooted in realms beyond this world, realms from which we in this world derive our values. Perhaps most importantly, the myth will prompt individuals whose lives are structured by its narrative, and by its often only semi-articulated practice, to look outward. Such people will be inspired by realities that do not simply echo their internal feelings or desires, but rather guide their lives and perceptions. The participants in a myth attend to something outside themselves and see themselves in a wider and more important context, one that is not chosen so much as simply there, beyond them, but also one that is elevating them as individuals into something grander, even something awesome. This inspirational attitude will be reinforced by the way the myths we are considering are typically embedded in communal rituals and practices. They are not matters of abstract theory or intellectual speculation so much as part of a communally held interweaving of practice, attitude, and thought about the world and our place within it.

The most ancient myth of which we have knowledge is the Mesopotamian Enuma Elish, probably dating from the early second millennium BC. Tiamat is the reptilian goddess of chaos and her husband is Apsu, the foundation of being and the source of order. They mate and produce the elder gods. But when Apsu is killed, Tiamat does nothing to help him. She also fills the world with reptilian monsters. The chief of the new gods, Marduk, cuts Tiamat into pieces and creates the world as we now know it, and rules over it. The myth and its accompanying ritual were held to represent the annual flooding of the Tigris and the Euphrates, and hence the salvific renewal of the creation of the world and its initial order, as well as the supremacy of Babylon, of which Marduk was the presiding deity. Jordan Peterson comments that aspects of this tale, transposed in various ways, can be found in ancient Egypt, in the Hebrew Bible, and in Christianity itself.[3]

Another striking early myth, and one actually based on some empirical phenomena, is that encapsulated in the recently discovered Nebra Sky Disc, dating once more from the first half of the second millennium BC. The disc pictures the sun and the moon

The Nebra Sky Disc

against a background of identifiable stars, all represented in luminous gold against a background of deep greenish bronze,

---

3. Peterson, "Three Forms of Meaning and the Management of Complexity," 33. See also Peterson, *Maps of Meaning*.

apparently encapsulating key moments in the solar year, and showing the celestial layout of the summer solstice, as observable from the Brocken mountain in Germany, near where the disc was found. At the bottom of the disc a boat, also in gold, is shown, with the oars of its crew represented. This is the boat in which in the thought of the time, as we know from other contemporary remains, the sun was carried below the sea each night, to sail on toward dawn and to be pulled up once more into the sky. On the surface, the myth may seem purely astronomical, as Stonehenge is sometimes understood, superficially in my view. For those who produced the disc and related objects—some of which have been found in graves—it is hard to believe that the setting and the rising of the sun did not symbolize or even impel the course of human life from its rising into the day of birth and on, into the darkness of the sea of death, and then to a resurrection *in valde mane*, in the early morning, as the Christian Easter account has it.[4]

Certainly, the tension between order and chaos, between darkness and light, between death and life, are fundamental in most mythical thinking, as is the notion that creation itself involves a dispersion of being or beings from an original One. There will also be the sense that our life here on earth is precariously balanced between contending forces of good and evil, between the organic and the inorganic, between life and death: "In Homer everything meshes, the whole world is a woof of 'umbilical cords'; the earthly, the heavenly world, animals, plants, elements, hearts of men, good, evil, death, life—that ripen, vanish and flower again. The mechanism of the gods performs nothing supernatural, nothing ex machina; it retains coherence, nothing else."[5] Thus the great Greek poet George Seferis on ancient Greek mythology, but I suspect its intimation of coherence is common to many others, and indeed to human feeling more generally about the earth we inhabit, when that world is not seen *more scientifico*. Of course, as

---

4. On the Nebra sky disc and related objects and carvings, including the Trundholm sun chariot, see Garrow and Wilkin, *The World of Stonehenge*, 133–50.

5. Seferis, *A Poet's Journal, Days of 1945–51*, 49.

readers of Homer will be aware, the balance and the coherence are not achieved without tension; it is a balance between contending forces and powers.

At this point it might be observed that the myths from some significant traditions and religions do not, on the face if it, see the world as created. Indeed, Karen Armstrong has made precisely this point in her book *Sacred Nature*.[6] What she says is no doubt true of her example of the Chinese notion of qi, which is central to much Chinese mythology, where there is no creator deity or moment of creation, such as we find in the Abrahamic monotheisms. Qi appears to be an unknowable basic force or pulse, neither spiritual nor material, not to be thought of as a god or a being, but something underlying and permeating everything. We can also think of the Chinese notion of yin and yang, ever oscillating and ever needing to be balanced. We can add to the idea of qi the later Chinese sense of Tao—a nameless source of all that there is, concealing more than it reveals, but embodied in everything, in a kind of perpetual dance in which individual things are or should be aiming to give up their narrow individuality to return to a renewed stillness.

The seminal Taoist thinker Lao Tzu put it like this: "There is a thing, confusedly formed, born before heaven and earth, silent and void. It stands alone and does not change, goes around and does not weary. It is capable of being the mother of the world. I know not its name, so I style it 'the way.'"[7] This thing—or perhaps non-thing, a reality beyond existence—is glossed by C. S. Lewis in *The Abolition of Man* as being the reality beyond all predicates, the abyss that was before the creator. It is the Way that the universe goes on, and to which we should conform our lives and ritual. Lewis points to the similarity between the Tao and the early Hindu Rta, "that great ritual or pattern of nature and supernature which is revealed alike in the cosmic order, the moral virtues and the ceremonial of the temple."[8] Not explicitly or literally Abrahamic,

---

6. Armstrong, *Sacred Nature*, 31–43.
7. Quoted in Kolakowski, *Religion*, 177.
8. Lewis, *The Abolition of Man*, 11.

indeed, but at a deep level this attitude is not so distant from the medieval Christian view that God is beyond human thought and conception, but nevertheless maintaining, sustaining, and enlivening the world.

Without pretending to any expertise in Chinese thought, we can note that neither qi nor Tao seem to imply that objects and creatures in the natural world are themselves gods, nor is the world itself divine, so long as we are looking at it as a system of purely physical forces as Newtonian and post-Newtonian physics would have it. It is rather that underpinning and sustaining the world as we see it, and as science analyses it, there is something non-material. What this is would not be revealed in the investigations of physics and biology. An imprecise but possibly helpful analogy to this strain of thought might be found in considering our attitudes to human persons. When we meet or love a person, what we meet or love is not the brute physical object before us—brain, muscle, sinew, blood, internal organs, and so on—but something—a self or a person, perhaps—that is incarnated in that corporeal object, and that will not be revealed by however detailed an investigation of that body and brain we might wish to undertake. The persons we are and deal with *are* embodied, but are not *just* bodies in the physical sense. As Leibniz argued long ago, if you could enlarge a brain so that you could walk round it, you will discover all sorts of physical movements and impulses, but you will never see a thought. And cutting up the brain will not be any more successful. You will just be left with mindless, unthinking stuff, however intricate and remarkable its structure. Brain science, for all its current sophistication, has not proved Leibniz wrong. The self, including its thoughts and feelings, eludes any such investigation and dissection, and so, despite their invocation in Chinese medicine, will qi or the Tao. And it is surely significant for our own natures, as well as cosmically, that in many of the myths we are considering God or gods take human form. Significantly too, Aristotle held so strong a view on the difference between the human person, enlivened and animated by psyche or soul, and unliving matter, that he did not consider the corpse of a dead person to be properly speaking human, as opposed to a merely material thing. Insights of this sort about the nature of the person and its relationship to the matter that encloses it, and about the potentially divine aspect of the person, underlie many religious myths—perhaps not surprisingly, given that from the purely scientific point of view, there is indeed a mystery about how matter in our human case becomes self-conscious and personal.

Even so, just as it is the person rather than the body that (or whom) we address in dealing with a human being, so it would be of qi or of the Tao. These realities are to be understood as sustaining the world and what is in it rather than reducible to the manifest form of things, even of the universe as a whole. As the person is not reducible to his or her body, considered as a piece of biological physiology, so too the world as a purely physical process would not be equivalent to qi or the Tao. If we are entitled to interpret qi and the Tao in this way, these ancient and apparently non-creatorial modes of thinking are not so far from the view of Thomas Aquinas that the universe is at every moment held in being by God's sustaining power in a manner invisible to empirical investigation. We could also refer to Calvin's evocative view that, while God dwells in a light inaccessible to us, "he irradiates the whole world in his splendour," the world being "the garment in which he, hidden in himself, appears in a manner visible to us."[9] This last thought resonates nicely with the idea that the Tao conceals as much as it reveals.

This is not a work of comparative mythology, nor am I claiming or intending to show that all myths can be shown to be consistent in every detail or to map easily on to each other. Indeed, one of my later proposals will be precisely to suggest that they are not straightforwardly mutually consistent. However, what I am suggesting is that in the myths I am interested in, there is characteristically a sense of the world as a whole, with forces or powers beyond the empirical, and of human and other life on earth as in some way sustained by and moving toward, or ideally aiming at, such powers.

9. Calvin, *Psalms 93–150*, 145.

The Place of Myth in Human Life

Often in discussions of this sort it is asserted that Buddhism is an exception to other religious myths, as an atheistic religion. But without saying more about Buddhism here than I am competent to do, it is surely the case that Buddhism is not an atheistic *materialism* of the reductively scientific sort. Even in the most austere formulations of Theravada Buddhism there is a sense of a universal process in which we are all involved spiritually, maybe through many lives, the cycle of birth and re-birth common to many Indian traditions. (Western "atheistic" Buddhists tend to play down the notion of reincarnation.) Nirvana, to which we, or the enlightened anyway, are tending, may be nothing or no *thing*, but it is certainly presented as a blissful state. It is something beyond the simple physical disintegration of death, which happens to every being, whether attaining Nirvana or not (being condemned to yet another passage on this earth, according to much Buddhist teaching). There is also the sense, common to most of the myths we will be thinking of, that most of human life is lived in a fallen or imperfect condition that needs some kind of religious redemption or enlightenment. All these central features of Buddhism would place it firmly into the category of myth I am interested in here, as would analogous aspects of qi and Tao, even if notions of a monotheist creation are not straightforwardly applicable to them. Actually, following Aquinas, we should recognize that the notion of a monotheistic creation, if taken in a literal, non-analogical sense, cannot properly be applied to Christianity either, or indeed to Islam or Judaism. It would also immediately fall foul of the Kantian antinomies.

But maybe it is not just on earth that things are balanced, albeit at times precariously. In myths of the divine realm itself there are sometimes contending deities, or of what we might think of as divisions, even tensions within the ultimate One. To say nothing of the Olympian and Norse pantheons, within Christianity we see in God both rulership and mercy, judgment and compassion, law and love, power and letting go, encompassed not just in a transition between the Old and the New Testaments, but in the doctrine of the Trinity, with different facets of the divinity manifested in the different "persons," on the face of it in some tension with each other. Does the divine kenosis, or "emptying out" of divinity, of which St. Paul speaks, not involve God himself in some sort of internal abdication or renunciation of majesty, which at the same time reveals the true meaning of divine power? From a human perspective it is hard not to see this as an eternal contrast between motives pulling in different directions, with their reconciliation at a deeper level, which is what is made articulate in the Christian myth of Trinity and incarnation. We can also note that despite what we have just called a transition between Old and New Testaments, in the New, the difference of tone notwithstanding, nothing of the Old is abrogated; the apparent conflict is somehow, even mysteriously, dissipated. In the book of Revelation, from the New Testament, Christ is both the Lion of Judah (of the Old, so to speak) and the Lamb "as if slaughtered" (of the New, but not unanticipated in the Old). The apparent contradiction may be resolved at a deep level; and we ourselves need both poles in our own lives, where there is continual tension between the need for the structures and institutions of a strong state and impartial justice, on the one hand, and ethical demands for the recognition of the rights of each individual, and mercy to the sinner, even where they may impede the application of what is needed for general peace and security.

Conflicts and tensions of this sort are frequently at the heart of the myths we are considering here. As Plato put it in *Phaedo* (70d–e), "it is a necessary law that everything which has an opposite is generated from that opposite, and from no other source," so beauty is generated from ugliness, right from wrong, and so on. We could add that Plato also thought that everything in this world—including beauty and ugliness, right and wrong—stemmed from some descent from a perfect One. So inherent in the picture he develops in his work—largely by means of myths—is an approach to the age-old question of why our world is fallen and imperfect, if, as the myths would have it, it emerges from a more perfect source. Myths are often ways of showing how these conundrums and opposites might be productive, and how the tensions might be resolved, as when, to take another example, Augustine speaks of the

The Place of Myth in Human Life

fall into sin as *felix culpa*, a happy fault, precisely because it is the enabling condition of Christ's incarnation. It may not be clear to the rational mind just how the existential questions and tensions are resolved, but their widespread prevalence in myth can suggest that they are not at a deep level irresolvable. They have to be lived with and through, and the myth will suggest ways of doing this. In other words, the widespread phenomenon of myths encapsulating accounts of our origins in a cosmic drama suggest that we should not rush into thinking that apparent difficulties and tensions at the cosmic level are necessarily fatal to a religious attitude to our existence.

We can think here of the Empedoclean doctrine that all derives from the age-old struggle between Love and Strife, of Pythagorean and Platonic accounts of descent from and return to the One, and of the Christian notion of original sin and consequent separation from God and paradise. And, to move to another great tradition, in the Sanskrit Vedas, creation costs the creator Prajapati great effort in which he becomes broken and needs to be reconstructed by the gods he has created, a ritual that is continually re-enacted throughout the year by Vedic priests. Of course, the Christian myth has Christ broken on the cross and then eaten by the faithful in the Eucharist, through which believers become one in Christ; Christ lives in them and they live in him. This should remind us of both Dionysus and Orpheus. Dionysus (or Bacchus) is torn to pieces and eaten by his followers, from which they receive his life and from which he too is resurrected. Orpheus descends into the underworld, is also torn to pieces by the Maenads before being swept up to heaven by Apollo, his father. Christ too descends into the underworld and, having risen, is eaten by his followers so that they might share in the divine life. Such notions are dimly evoked by the ancient Greek Eleusinian mysteries, in which the uninitiated (the un-baptized?) descend into a cave representing Hades or the underworld, and then, like Perspehone in the myth, come up from the infernal depth to a new life on earth. Similarly, the Bacchic rites described by Euripides in his play of that name suggest that human beings can share in a divine ecstasy by engaging in ceremonies of ritual violence. E. R. Dodds refers to this "eating of God in the shape of man" as a "dreadful sacrament," which could suggest that contemporary Christians have become somewhat insensitive to the scandalously atavistic nature of the Eucharist.[10] Equally it might suggest something deep about the relationship between our nature and the divine, as it did to St. Augustine, who wrote that in Christ "the Creator has become a creature ... and has gathered us up into himself, to become one single man, head and body."[11] At all events, the myths we have been referring to here all point in their different ways to cosmic struggle, separation, loss of an original unity or balance, and then a sacrificial discipline of return to or re-absorption in the original unity.

Peterson says that we are not to think of these myths as theories of objective existence, but rather as imaginative roadmaps to being. They will have emerged as a result of our continual reflecting on ourselves and patterns of our behavior which have proved adaptive. In this process they will have taken on representational form, in narratives, dramas and rituals, in which the behavior underlying them becomes clothed in concrete imagery.[12] Are they true? Could they be true? Obviously, as already noted, they are not true, if by true we mean correspondence of logically structured pictures or propositions to the facts envisaged in the *Tractatus*. Those pictures, and the propositions that encapsulate them, can, as Wittgenstein himself observed, "express nothing that is higher,"[13] and the same could be said of the empirically ascertainable facts of history and the social sciences, where once again statements are held to be true or false as they accord or don't accord with evidence available through observation and available to any dispassionate enquirer, prescinding from any mythical overlay or interpretation.

But, as Peterson himself has observed (in conversation), the notion of truth is not so narrow: true, like a steadfast heart; true

---

10. Dodds, *The Greeks and the Irrational*, 278.
11. Augustine, "Commentary on Psalm 85," 1176–77.
12. See Peterson, "Three Forms of Meaning and the Management of Complexity," 33. See also Peterson, *Maps of Meaning*.
13. Wittgenstein, *Tractatus Logico-Philosophicus*, prop 6.42 (p. 145).

as the arrow flies. Much contemporary philosophy, particularly in Anglo-American academic circles, is dominated Tarski's theory of truth (and the developments of it by Donald Davidson). Alfred Tarski, a twentieth-century Polish logician, analyzed truth in terms of sentences being true if (and only if) there was a state of affairs to which the sentence referred. Thus, sentence "p" is true if and only if p, where p is the state of affairs being mentioned in the sentence "p." To take the example that is always given, the sentence "Snow is white" is true if and only if snow is white.

Like Wittgenstein's picture theory, Tarski presents a restricted notion of truth, covering only those cases where there is a potential logically structured correspondence between what is asserted to be true and some fact or facts in the world, usually of an observable sort. For all the validity and power of an approach like Tarski's, particularly when used, as Tarski himself advocated, in conjunction with logically formalized languages, if it is taken to be a complete account of the notion of truth, it illegitimately cuts off other and equally valid, and often more humane, applications of truth. A true friend; the truth in *Antigone*; the truth in Glenn Gould's playing of Bach or in Sokolov's of Chopin, which has little to do with the "correctness" (or not) of the musician's following of the score, but which gets us to *see*, and not just hear, what in a sense is behind the physical sounds. (There is a story told by an eventually admiring pupil of Sokolov's, that having heard her play a piece by Schumann, correctly as far as the notes went, the great pianist buried his head in his hands, uttering "You know nothing about Schumann." No doubt an exaggeration, and probably unfair, but any musically sensitive listener will understand what Sokolov was getting at, a level of truth about Schumann's music that goes beyond what we might call the factual faithfulness of the notes played to the written score.) Mythical truth is truth of the heart, an arrow flying to its target. We can think here of the biblical expression "living in the truth," which suggests that the truth in question is not one of purely factual or intellectual significance; it is a truth that inextricably carries with it not just understanding and belief in an abstract sense, but also commitment to a way of life, in a community of like-minded believers. As Pascal reminded us, and we have mostly forgotten, there is *esprit de finesse* as well as *esprit de géométrie*.

As far as truth goes, above the deliverances of sense and reason, there are the intimations of the heart, the heart being that element in our make-up that underpins and guides our attitudes, sensitivity, values, and ultimately our behavior, as self-conscious beings making our individual and collective ways through the world. It is the heart that the myths to which Peterson refers educate, and it is in terms of responses from the heart that they are verified, seen as true. It is to the heart that they speak, filled as they often are with wisdom and insight gained over long centuries of experience and human interaction. In life we learn through experience, but fortunately we are not on our own in this. We are only the latest in a line of many generations and of a culture we inherit. Myths, then, are narratives that connect and join what might otherwise be detached experiences and facts. They unfold in a dynamic way a sense of who and what we are, speaking of meanings beyond us, meanings in which we are intimately involved, but that are handed down to us, and that also specify ways of behaving. We fall into these stories, which we sense as being composed by mythologists who are "tuned in" to worlds beyond our own everyday landscapes. They are human, but in the case of specifically religious myths, more than human. At least, that is how they appear to those who see them as divinely inspired, which is something I am about to argue we should not reject out of hand, given the universality of themes in the myths, to which we have just referred, and what often seems in them to be a preternatural, if not supernatural, wisdom and insight.

We might quibble at this point, about the power that myths hold on us when we are captivated by them. Some will no doubt recall Hamlet's complaint about the actor falsely weeping for Hecuba when he fails to acknowledge things in life that ought to move him.

> For Hecuba!
> What's Hecuba to him, or he to Hecuba

The Place of Myth in Human Life

> That he should weep for her? . . . Yet I
> A dull and muddy-mettled rascal, peak,
> Like John-a-dreams, unpregnant of my cause,
> And can say nothing.
>
> (*Hamlet*, Act II, Sc II)

The criticism would be that what we are given in a myth, such as the Homeric myth, but perhaps also in the myths of the great religions, is not just unreal, but also something that for some people provokes far more lively an emotional reaction than do the actual tragedies, deaths, and misfortunes they encounter in their own lives and in the lives of those around them. There may be some truth here, in that there can be factitious and sentimental dimensions to our responses to art and literature, including myth and indeed in religion itself, where hard-hearted believers are all awash with religious sentiment even as they neglect the calls of those around them.

But there is another way of looking at this. Many people find it hard to respond emotionally to what is before them. Their feelings appear to dry up even in the face of terrible events. Maybe it is in art and literature, in Shakespeare and Rembrandt, say, that the feelings they know not how to express or articulate actually find an outlet and what is suppressed in their lives up to that point is actually opened up, channeled and given release. And not just in art, but perhaps more deeply and imperceptibly in communal myths, which structure the life and religion of a people.

Art and myth not only teach us how to feel about the realities we are confronted with, but can also release feelings and reactions pent up within, frozen as it were in an internal stasis. Berlioz is recorded by the dramatist Auguste Barbier as remaining still and apparently unmoved at the burial of a friend, but dissolving into heartfelt tears when he returned to his room and read passages from Shakespeare. In Barbier's words, "aesthetic emotion provoked the catharsis that real loss had been unable to do."[14] Shakespeare thus gave him the means to react, unfroze what had been the ice within. Thus it is, or can be, with myth, and particularly because

---

14. See Bloom, *Berlioz in Time*, 142.

myths typically deal with situations and feelings of universal relevance, and are often heard in solemn or ritualistic settings, as well as involving the participant in related liturgies, ceremonies, and practices.

The experience of those past generations and of our culture is thus transmitted to us in the myths we learn, or did learn, as children, and then see developed in our own adult experience. It is, of course, in the way that these myths do or do not seem true to what we are that the myths themselves live or die or are transformed. Probably to most people in the contemporary West the Christian myth no longer seems true to what they are, though this may be more because they no longer live by that myth and no longer have any lived experience of its meaning, rather than because of the myth lacking truth. At any rate, Nietzsche, something of a false prophet when it came to myth, was certainly right when in 1871 he observed that in the face of the Enlightenment and scientific approaches to knowledge, "myth, the essential prerequisite of every religion, is already paralysed."[15] He actually said paralyzed *everywhere*, a pardonable exaggeration if one simply looks at the contemporary Western modernity that Nietzsche, despite himself, did not a little to bring about.

Even if we live, or think we live, in a demythologized world, this has not been the case with the majority of peoples in the past, or indeed with the majority of humankind now. Some may insist on restricting what we are allowed to contemplate to the barely factual, to truths as envisaged in Wittgenstein's picture theory, but, as we have suggested, this would be a very restricted sense of "truth." And in repudiating or cutting ourselves off from the myths that have captivated the minds of so many for so long, we will also be cutting ourselves off from vital and even life-enhancing sources of truth. In the next chapter, by reference to a famous encounter between C. S. Lewis and J. R. R. Tolkien we will attempt to show why this might be so.

---

15. Nietzsche, *The Birth of Tragedy*, section 18, 111.

3

Addison's Walk
A Story of Two Mythologists

IN HIS BIOGRAPHY OF C. S. Lewis,[1] A. N. Wilson tells us that when Lewis finally embraced Christianity in 1931, a nocturnal conversation and walk with J. R. R. Tolkien and Hugo Dyson along Addison's Walk in Magdalen College, Oxford was the turning point. The conversation turned on the significance of myth. Lewis could not see "how the life and death of Someone Else (whoever he was) 2000 years ago could help us here and now—except as his *example* helped us." It is as if Lewis was looking at Jesus in the same way as he might have looked at Socrates or Julius Caesar, as historically factual characters, who might have influenced us in various ways, as having made their mark on our own time through their diffused historical influence, but whose time had passed, and who could have no personal connection to us, or involvement with us. Tolkien took issue with what he took to be a failure of feeling and imagination on Lewis's part. When Lewis came across myths of divine figures who die and rise again, as is the case of the three

---

1. Wilson, *C. S. Lewis: A Biography*, 125–27. I have drawn heavily in this section and later on Wilson's account and on the quotations he gives. References to the quotations can be found in Wilson's book.

Tolkien mentioned (Balder, Adonis, and Bacchus), he was deeply affected, even though he knew that Balder, Adonis, and Bacchus were not, properly speaking, historical figures. Not only were they not historical figures, but the myths in which these characters figured were what we have called "dead," no longer part of any actual religious tradition in the contemporary world. Nevertheless, as Lewis himself said, commenting on Tolkien's position, he could still "feel the myth as profound and suggestive of meanings beyond my grasp even tho' I could not say in cold prose 'what it meant.'"

We can go beyond the somewhat learned diet of examples Lewis referred to in talking of myths as profound and suggestive of meanings beyond our grasp. In David Matthews's opera, *Anna*, set to a libretto by Roger Scruton, Peter the tormented anti-hero is struggling to come to terms with the death of his father under the Czech secret police and also with the way that the old culture his father stood for seems to have been lost after the Velvet Revolution rather than being restored, as the opponents of the communist dictatorship had hoped. Being told by his friend Marta, who represents a kind of wisdom, that "in the days when God existed" (in communist times, in other words), his father taught Christian forgiveness, Peter scornfully replies that this message is no more than a fairy tale we no longer need. Marta patiently replies, "in fairy tales there is also truth: so your father taught."[2]

Significant, I think, because it was fairy tales, among other things, that gave people in that drear time something to cling on to when everything they believed in and hoped was cynically smashed and trampled on by the communists. Fairy tales in Czechoslovakia: maybe *Rusalka*, the tale of a water-nymph who longs for human life and love, but whose pursuit of her end leads to a tragic death for her lover and a spectral half-life for herself (note how once again human life is seen as fraught with pain, sin, and contradiction, though also with a vein of nobility, love, and

---

2. Roger Scruton (libretto) and David Matthews (music), the opera *Anna* (formerly *An Angel Passes*). Libretto published by Faber Music 2020, Act II, Sc IV. The opera has been performed in a piano reduction and also in an orchestral concert version at the Grange Festival, June 2023.

compassion, and note too the moving, elevated, and imaginatively vivifying way in which Dvorak set the tale to music); or maybe the feelings running through Smetana's *Ma Vlast*, to the Czechs a scenario embodying and expressing much of their suppressed national consciousness. (*Ma Vlast* means "My Country.") To Czech ears, Smetana's music conveys a sense of a reality more real and more genuine and more true than the fallen world in which we are oppressed by the universal law of nature that tells us that survival and reproduction are all, and that in that world, as the Czechs knew all too well even in the nineteenth century, the strong dominate and the weak suffer what they must. Such is the power of the music that something of this will be conveyed to non-Czechs who listen to it with the attention it demands.[3]

Going beyond *Ma Vlast* and *Anna*, in his book *The Soul of the World* Scruton, *in propria persona*, argues that the myth of origin, specifically that of the fall into sin, "records a deep truth about the human psyche," though going on to suggest that we should not look at it in historical terms, as if it were telling us things about what happened in or before human prehistory. It is about something *always* true, "a revelation of present realities," but expressed through the medium of a deep and "primeval encounter with the order of nature." (He refers here to Wagner's *Ring* cycle, and specifically to the Norns weaving the rope of destiny, as similarly expressing deep truths about human nature.) He goes on to say that myths and stories that have become embedded in a culture are

> ways of tying the *Lebenswelt* (i.e., the world in which we live, rather than the skeletal, meaning-eviscerated world of natural science) to nature. This does not mean that the

---

3. On the subject of *Ma Vlast* and what it means to Czechs: thanks to Norwegian radio, of all things, who broadcast the performance, there is an extraordinary recording of that work from 1939 conducted by Vaclac Talich in the Rudolfinum in Prague. The odiously triumphant Germans are strutting all around, but the orchestra plays on, with huge eruptions of applause after each movement, not just because of the fact that it was being played, but even more because of the *way* it was being played. Talich himself, an honorable man as well as a notable musician, suffered later under the communists as he had suffered earlier under the Nazis.

stories are simply pleasing fictions. They have been clung to and repeated by people in their moments of adversity. They are the surviving fragments of texts that persecuted communities have refused to relinquish in their hour of need, since they contain the answer to suffering and the vision of the order beyond disorder—the order that reveals itself, when the covenant collapses.[4]

Among other things, Scruton is clearly referring here to the is way dissidents in communist times clung on to the old myths of religion as a source of hope, as true in the Czechoslovakia depicted in *Anna* as in Poland, though less well known in the wider world. But the scourge of powerlessness and meaninglessness may oppress people just as much under global capitalism as under obvious political persecution. The individual may feel just as helpless and frustrated. The covenant may collapse there too, as we see in *Anna*. So the need for myth can be strong, even when "freedom" comes. There is, though, a danger that the myth that comes to fill the void in such circumstances may be a false utopianism, which would promise a heaven on earth, a world free from capitalism, racism, sexism, and all other ills, real or imagined, rather than consolation from another dimension altogether. The Czechs depicted in *Anna* knew all too well the abyss into which utopian politics plunges those unlucky enough to experience it.

One lesson we can take from the religious and cultural myths of the past is that they give access to a non-empirical, unconditioned world, and at the same time a critique of the world in which we actually live. In one way or another, the world of actual events is shown to be inevitably a vale of tears, but combined with this is a vision of a better world that is our true home. In C. S. Lewis's later work there is a very strong sense of how intimations of this better world enter into our lives here and now, but not so as to give us the illusion that we could actually attain that world in this life. As we are shown in the book of Revelation, the New Jerusalem descends from heaven, rather than being made by us here and now, a message that can be found in other terms in other religious

---

4. See Scruton, *The Soul of the World*, 107–8 and 184.

traditions. The fact that so many religiously minded leaders have taken Revelation as implying that they could themselves build the New Jerusalem in a fit of revolutionary slate cleaning only goes to show how fatally easy it is to misinterpret a sacred text, with catastrophic results. As we will stress in due course, divine revelations are always mediated through human vessels, which should lead to caution in their interpretation; they can never be the whole or the absolute truth.

But why, when it came to Christianity, did Lewis's imaginative powers initially desert him? Why did he react as a logical positivist empiricist would have done? Why did he not at first understand, as he later recorded, and as Tolkien urged on him, that "the story of Christ is simply a true myth: a myth working on us in the same way as the others, but with this tremendous difference that it *really happened*: and one must be content to accept it in the same way"? I am about to suggest that their really happening, in the way that Caesar crossed the Rubicon, or more accurately, their *not* happening in that way, may not be crucial to the underlying truth of the myths Lewis in his pre-Christian state was so moved by. Indeed, it may actually be that the very mundane historicity of the existence of Jesus impedes our understanding of that passage of chronos time as something endowed with eternal or kairotic significance. And yet the reality of God in some way and at some time entering the world, *actually* doing so and then rising again, is pivotal to the mythical truth encapsulated in the tales of Balder, Adonis, and Bacchus. For if these myths of divine entry into our fallen human world do not, in a real way, represent something of the truth of the universe, of God or gods in some way entering our world, then they are just tales, just fantasies, just make-believe, mere fairy stories in a derogatory sense. The scandal of the Christian myth is that it has God *actually* entering the world at a specific time in the most prosaic and mundane way, as a beggar in an insignificant and down-trodden corner of the world, and then departing it as a despised criminal. In this way, the Christian myth, of these things actually happening, will be seen to underpin the truth Lewis and others find in the stories of Balder, Adonis, and Bacchus.

The Prism of Truth

An evocative comment on what I am calling the scandal of the Christian myth can be found buried within the Pauline chapel in the Vatican, in the complementary pair of frescoes there by Michelangelo, the *Conversion of Paul* and the *Crucifixion of Peter*.[5] Paul receives his revelation through grace, and as he has it in his Letter to the Galatians 1:11–12, receives it "neither of man, nor was I taught it." It was conveyed to him immediately from heaven by the now resurrected Jesus Christ speaking directly to him and casting him to the ground in a flash of miraculous light. This was not the flesh-and-blood Jesus Christ, whom Peter knew as a man, and indeed denied. Peter, in Michelangelo's fresco is represented as looking from his inverted cross despairingly, if not angrily at the spectator, and also at the Paul on the wall opposite. It is as if he is peering into the unknown, uncertain of his salvation. Michelangelo's Paul (a self-portrait, some have argued) is blinded and on the ground where he has fallen, with his entourage and horse in disarray. Unlike Peter, he is bathed in the light from Christ and the angels above him, who are apparently invisible to the other figures in the scene. So the grace-inspired but blinded Paul is rock-like in his faith, a faith others are unaware of except as the source of terror and chaos. The huge bolting horse can be seen as a nod to Plato's doctrine in the *Phaedrus* of the two horses we sit astride in life, the impassioned horse fighting the rational horse. Does Michelangelo want us to see Paul's impassioned horse careering away with Saul's terrestrial passions, and indeed with Michelangelo's own baser instincts, which would certainly be consistent with the poetry he was writing at the time? By contrast, the Peter opposite, who actually knew Christ as a human figure, is still in doubt, even in denial once more, even at the very moment of his martyrdom, needing the final shedding of blood to solidify his faith. Much to the point, Michelangelo himself in his crucifixion drawing in the Isabella Stewart Gardner Museum in Boston, quotes Dante, "there they do not think of how much blood it costs" (*Paradiso*, XXIX, 91), something Peter is about to understand in his own body.

---

5. *The Conversion of Paul* is reproduced on p. 99 below.

Michelangelo's pair of frescoes can be seen as in a part as a comment, perhaps veiled, on the Lutheran Reformation and Michelangelo's own association with Vittoria Colonna and the socalled Spirituali, loyal Catholics who were nevertheless in secret sympathy with the reformers' critique of the Roman church. Peter being given the keys of the church by Christ would be the normal iconographic pendant to Paul's conversion. Such an image would be taken naturally as an assertion of the scripturally endorsed supremacy of the pope, Peter's successor, and of the Roman church as the vehicle of salvation. It was just this that Luther, with his grace-inspired Pauline theology, was questioning. Salvation is an individual matter, secured not by works or gifts to the Roman church, or indeed by the teaching of men, however elevated in a church hierarchy, but by only the gift of grace. It was this grace that Paul received on the road to Damascus, and that Peter is about to be given belatedly through his martyrdom. To pair Paul's conversion with a representation of a somewhat equivocal Peter being bound to his cross, especially at the heart of the Roman papacy, was a dramatic statement at the time, just when the aggressively pro-papal counter-Reformation was gathering pace in Rome.

From our point of view, equally relevant as a comment on the impact of Michelangelo's frescoes is the statement of his soulmate Vittoria Colonna, to the effect that we humans struggle "among shadows and figures, bound by a thousand ropes in a blind alley."[6] The Christian myth is indeed walking among shadows and figures. To see God in the man Christ, who walked in Galilee and Jerusalem two thousand years ago is, as Lewis suggested, in some ways more problematic than taking into one's heart the frankly mythical tales of Balder, Adonis, and Dionysus. This is surely part of what Michelangelo is intimating in his frescoes: Paul infused with divine grace, but blind to the world, and Peter with his eyes open, seemingly struggling with doubt and even anger at the moment of

---

6. The quotation from Vittoria Colonna can be found in Paolo Carloni's *Come in uno specchio*, 164. (English translation in the same volume, as *Through a Glass Darkly*; the Colonna quotation is translated on p. 399). In my interpretation of Michelangelo's works I have drawn on Carloni's work.

death, and this even after years of close personal knowledge of the man Jesus.

In the Addison's Walk conversation, Tolkien averred that the "doctrines" that emerged or were extracted from the Christian myth are less true than the myth itself. We may have reservations about this; after all, the full meaning of the Christian myth, ideas about the incarnation and the Trinity, only emerged gradually, after several centuries of learned doctrinal debate. Nevertheless, we can accept that the truth that underlies the myth is too large and too all-embracing for the finite mind to grasp or express fully, particularly perhaps if squeezed into doctrines formulated in rationalistic or philosophical form, which is part of the reason that the divinity reveals itself to us humans in myths, a point to which we will shortly return. Lewis's initial reaction to Tolkien's apparent obfuscation was that it amounts to "breathing a lie through silver."[7] But for Tolkien, the opposite is the case. Myths, especially the old and most venerable ones, are traces of the human capacity, before the fall, to see into the life of things. We are operating here in the region of the heart, our spirit that of *finesse*, of what is inside us in our deepest feelings, rather than that of *géométrie* or of empirical observation. Perhaps we could gloss this point with the observation that, at the deepest level, Tolkien's own great myth is not about battles and struggles in the physical world, but about battles and struggles in the hearts and minds of its characters—something evident in the written text, but somewhat missing, maybe unavoidably, from the film. At the very least, Tolkien's thought about ancient myths, which as we will later see is repeating the views of Marsilio Ficino and Plato on this topic, should lead us to question the presumption of the rationalist that our recent scientific progress is in all respects progress *simpliciter*.

---

7. Quoted by Wilson, *C.S. Lewis: A Biography*, 219.

4

From Myth to Science
A Popperian Analysis

> Yes, they have gone; all beauty
> Everything higher is gone with them,
> All color, all the tones of life.
> To us remains only a de-souled world.
> Torn away from the flood of time,
> The gods have risen to the heights of Pindus.
> Whatever lives in song immortal
> Must in life go under.
> —Schiller, from "The Gods of Greece" (author's translation)

IT IS ONE OF Karl Popper's most intriguing insights that the history of what we regard as science is a history of the transformation of ideas from mythical untestability to empirical testability. But unlike many of those who pronounce on a or the transition, as they see it, from *mythos* to *logos* (irrational to rational, in other words), Popper is no despiser of myth per se. "Historically speaking all—or very nearly all—scientific theories originate from myths, and a myth may contain important anticipations of scientific theories."[1]

---

1. Popper, *Conjectures and Refutations*, 38.

The reason that Popper thinks that scientific theories often originate from myths is that he believes that all scientific theories begin with some speculative hunch as to how things are. They do not begin with observation, as many believe, because observation always has to be guided by some idea of what one is observing, and why the things one is observing might be worth spending time and effort on observing. And the guiding idea of a scientific theory might well, as Popper says, be mythical or originate in a myth.

Of course, Popper, being a passionate admirer of science, is keen to differentiate science from myth, and it must be admitted that, without dismissing myth, in comparing the two he will give science the palm. Thus, as is well known, he is fiercely critical of the claims of psychoanalysis, in the manner of Freud and Adler, to be scientific. It has, he says, no stronger claim than the Homeric stories to scientific status, which is because its ideas are not empirically testable. Adler's ideas and Freud's "epic of the Ego, the Superego, and the Id describe some facts, but in the manner of myths. They contain most interesting psychological suggestions, but not in a testable form."[2] Those who have heard only that Popper was a remorseless critic of Freud may be surprised to discover that he thinks Freud makes most interesting psychological observations, and no doubt he would say the same of Homer. People who knew Popper confirm that he was actually fascinated by some of Freud's ideas, considering them suggestive in understanding people, but they were not *scientific*. Once again, unlike the logical positivists, Popper was by no means dismissive of "unscientific" thinking as such. But he objected strongly to the claim made by Freud and his followers that their ideas amounted to a scientific approach to personality and psychology. They did not, because the Freudians never specified what would count as evidence against their theories. And crucially—and here Popper is closer to the logical positivists than he might like to appear—Popper does think that the scientific method, of testing hypotheses objectively and rigorously against objectively available empirical evidence, does represent an advance in both thought *and* civilization.

2. Popper, *Conjectures and Refutations*, 38.

From Myth to Science

We can see Greek thought in the sixth and fifth centuries BC as a stepping-stone from the gods of Olympus to the fully fledged empirical science that has dominated in our culture since the sixteenth and seventeenth centuries, if, as Popper did, we consider the way the pre-Socratics differed from their Homeric predecessors. The Homeric myths, like many others before and later, try to explain human life and the natural phenomena we are surrounded by in terms of various divine agents controlling, directing, and interfering in events here on earth. Thus, we have the pantheon of Zeus, Poseidon, Hades, and their lesser companions, not only contending with each other but also influencing events here: Zeus the heavens, sky, and storms, Poseidon the sea, Hades the underworld, and so on. Where the pre-Socratics made an advance scientifically speaking on these personalized explanations was that they looked for abstract and impersonal regularities governing the world as a whole.

Thus, Thales famously saw water and its transformations as somehow underlying the whole world, Anaximander that some elementary "boundless" element or stuff was governed by necessity to produce the world as we know it, Heraclitus that everything is in constant flux, constantly re-balancing opposites, Parmenides that there is some unchanging essence that we perceive misleadingly as the phenomenal world, Pythagoras that number is at the root of everything, Empedocles that love and strife contending together for ever mixed and unmixed the four basic elements of earth, air, fire, and water, and so on.

In addition to producing generalized and largely impersonal accounts of the cosmos, according to Popper, in criticizing their theories the pre-Socratics went a long way toward the critical rationalist approach he so admired, even, he claims, inventing it. They thus paved the way for "our Western civilization, the only civilization which is based on science (though of course not upon science alone)."[3] Popper's qualification here is significant in the way it distances him from the scientism of the logical positivists, but the sentiment is still striking enough. And, reflecting on the

---

3. Popper, *Conjectures and Refutations*, 151.

transitions between the different pre-Socratics, he claims that apart from the Pythagoreans they were not concerned to preserve their favored ideas as quasi-religious doctrines, beyond criticism. Instead, starting with Thales, they tolerated criticism, and even encouraged it, which is what in Popper's view the attitude of critical rationalism amounts to. And so we have the amazing plurality of doctrines over a few generations. Critical examination of theories was already alive in sixth and fifth century BC Greece, though it died away with the classical world, not to be revived until Galileo in the seventeenth century. Nor was the critical examination of theories in ancient Greece yet a fully-fledged *scientific* method. There was not yet a tradition of submitting one's theories to empirical testing and potential and actual refutation through such testing.[4]

We can see this very clearly in the case of Leucippus and Democritus, the ancient Greek atomists, who strikingly anticipated much of seventeenth-century scientific thought. They held that the world consisted of atoms, indivisible particles moving around in empty space according to necessary laws. The objects of everyday experience and we ourselves are simply complexes of these atoms, which hold together for a time before breaking up and entering into other complexes, and so forming new objects. But like many of their pre-Socratic contemporaries, the atomists combined their beliefs about the fundamental nature of the cosmos with ideas about how life should be lived, in their case very strongly so. Ancient atomism went along with an attitude of acceptance of what had to be. This attitude of Leucippus and Democritus was refined by the somewhat later Epicurus into a claim that on death all that happened was that the atoms that had made us conscious simply

---

4. Popper himself actually downplays the significance of observation and experiment in science. He considers this crucial aspect of the scientific method to be of real significance only as it features in a practice of critical argument, which he sees already in the pre-Socratics, excluding the Pythagorean school, which he regards as insistent on preserving a doctrine. (See Popper, *Conjectures and Refutations*, 150–53.) Nevertheless, it remains true that testing through systematic observation and experiment is a key aspect of what we think of as the scientific method, and this aspect is not to found in the pre-Socratics.

From Myth to Science

take up different configurations, at which point our experience would cease. Therefore, there being nothing to experience after we die, there is nothing to fear.

In his poem *Aubade*, Philip Larkin scornfully dismisses the Epicurean belief that the rational person should not fear what cannot be experienced, and so should confront the fact of death with equanimity. For Larkin, it was just this abyss of non-feeling, this cessation of experience, that was truly terrifying.[5] Larkin's unstoic attitude to the very phenomenon that fueled Epicurus's stoicism is a way of underlining the extent to which even in a comparatively spare myth, such as that of ancient atomism, the attitudes enshrined in it go way beyond the empirical basis. The Roman Lucretius followed Epicurus in the main, adding the idea that tales of gods were invented by our ancestors to explain things they could not understand, and hence were afraid of. There may be a creator, but such a being is utterly remote and uninterested in human affairs. "True piety consists in the power to contemplate the universe with a quiet mind."[6] But in all of this, the doctrine itself and its intimate connection with a philosophy of life, Leucippus, Democritus, Epicurus, and Lucretius were not in the modern sense scientists.

Although what they said did draw on certain aspects of the observable world, the ancient atomists had no idea of what the atoms they spoke of actually were, or how to observe them. No more than the other pre-Socratics with their speculations, the ancient atomists had no evidence of a scientific sort for the atoms they postulated. Atoms became part of actual science only in the seventeenth century and subsequently, corpuscles measurable and in a sense observable. The atomic theory of John Dalton, which revealed the atomic structure of the chemical elements in the nineteenth century, was indeed a triumph of empirical science, but the ancient idea that atoms—or what were regarded as atoms—were indivisible and fundamental did not survive that long into the twentieth century. Quantum theory showed that atoms, far from

---

5. Larkin, "Aubade," in *Collected Poems*, 208–9.
6. Lucretius, *Of the Nature of the Universe*, 208.

being the ultimate and indivisible constituents of matter, were found to be divisible, and to be made up of even smaller particles. Doubts have since emerged as to whether the ultimate constituents of matter are particles at all, as opposed to waves or entities of a quite unknown sort, neither waves nor particles, but areas in space that exude forces of various sorts. Talk of quantum entanglement points to some of the difficulties without solving them, beyond suggesting that deep down reality is very different from anything resembling the atoms of the ancient or even later atomists. It would not be unfair to say that the successes of corpuscularism over the past three to four hundred years notwithstanding, very little is now left of anything remotely resembling the atomism of ancient Greece and Rome.

Nevertheless, the story of atomism from the ancient Greeks to Dalton in the nineteenth century is one of a myth gradually becoming empirically scientific. The atomism of the classical world was mythical not just because it produced no empirically testable predictions, which is what has come to be seen as the hallmark of a genuinely scientific theory. Rather more important is the way that the atomism of the ancient world was part of a metaphysical worldview, one replete with ethical and quasi-religious overtones and undertones. Leucippus and Democritus were trying to find a way through some of the big pre-Socratic questions, as to the ultimate reality (or not) of change, and also as to whether the universe should be seen as One or as a complex of many things. For the atomists, the universe was both changing and unchanging. Its ultimate constituents did not change, but the complexes they formed part of for a time did. And the atoms were all of one type, all one, though again the things that groups of them formed were many and different. On to this basic picture of the world, which united many apparently conflicting insights, Epicurus and Lucretius painted not just an agnostic or even atheistical philosophy (in what concerns us, nothing but atoms and the void), but also a philosophy of life. Do not fear death. Live so as to avoid exciting the passions—too much movement and friction in the atoms that make us up will bring us only pain. Modern scientists may share some of the metaphysical, religious, and ethical attitudes of the ancient atomists, but what we might call this mythical carapace is not part of the physical theory espoused by Lavoisier, Dalton, Maxwell, and their twentieth- and twenty-first-century descendants. Empirical science is shorn of its mythical and moral implications, leaving us only the measurable and the observable.

The success of modern science in its own terms is precisely because it has now shed its mythical and, up to a point, its metaphysical elements. Its validity and its strength arise from its independence from humanity. It tells us how the world operates in isolation from what we feel about it. But its strength is also its limitation. It abstracts from the way the world affects us, and from how we react to it.

"In our life alone does Nature live": thus, in the *Dejection Ode*, did Coleridge stress the way that the world lives in us and through us, and becomes perceived and felt in a conscious and self-conscious way. Or, as Rilke wonders in the *Ninth Duino Elegy*, whether the purpose the earth has for us is that we should articulate even mundane notions, such as house, bridge, spring, gate, window, and so on. In doing so we will give these things a reality they would never otherwise achieve, making them delight in their enhanced reality.[7] Rilke is echoing the doctrine dear to Schelling and the romantics, that we as human beings articulate the meanings concealed within the physical world, but also in a way anticipating what is implicit in the anthropic principle modestly understood.

We, as creatures of the natural world and its evolution, are attuned to it from its origin, and this potential for a conscious attunement, which is realized in us, must have been present in the universe from its very beginning, from the Big Bang, or whatever. And, mindful of the Kantian antinomy, if we do not believe in a Big Bang, but in a universe with no beginning, then this potential must be there always and forever. Either way, it would follow that physics, which can give no satisfactory account of the emergence of life from purely non-living material, let alone of how matter can

7. Rilke, *Duino Elegies*, 85.

become conscious, for all its undoubted strength, must be seen as an abstraction from the whole. Physics is true enough in explaining the domain of the inorganic and unconscious, but even there it glosses over potentialities that must be there for life and conscious beings like us to have emerged out of what, on the face of it and in its early stages, was a wholly inorganic universe.

But we are here and, as products of evolution, we are in large part attuned to the world in which and in conformity with which we have been formed (or we would not have survived even for the time that we have survived). Our being attuned to the world means that our inner being, as a German idealist such as Schelling might have put it, is ready to feel, express, and articulate aspects of nature that would not otherwise have been disclosed. Highly pertinent here is the way our perception of nature unites and connects aspects of the world and of experience that the atomizing and objectivizing investigations of the natural sciences tend to keep apart. And in our attuned and attuning disclosing of nature and the world, we are not only throwing light on that world, we are also expressing something of our own essence.

Such a thought is memorably articulated in the Qur'an: "It is He [Allah] who spread out the earth, placed firm mountains and rivers on it, and made two of every kind of fruit. He draws the veil of night over the day. There truly are signs in this for people who reflect" (13.3). The reflection being spoken of here is not the analytical reflection we find in natural science, but a complementary mode of reflection, when we simply regard the world and nature in its immensity, and also in its minute, unimaginable intricacy and delicacy, with awe and wonder. The scientific explanations stand, but they do not capture aspects of the world and attitudes to it that come to us with an immediate and at times overwhelming power, nor are such feelings, which come to us almost unbidden, invalidated by the scientific explanations. It is as if, as inferred by Muhammad and Rilke, we are here on earth precisely to have such feelings and to reveal the wonder of existence and nature.

Finding a gloomy immensity in a mountain range is not invalidated by knowledge of how mountains might have formed. The pristine luminous purity of the Evening Star is not contradicted by the fact that it is actually the planet Venus, an orb largely of gas and brute matter. Nor is the drama of the dawn and day gradually dispersing the half-light in an eventually overwhelming symphony of light in any way cancelled out by knowledge of the earth's own rotation and orbit round a medium sized and astronomically insignificant star (as we are told). And the intricacy and sheer delicacy of a spider's web or the sheer precision of the cells that go to make up an animal's eye are hardly made less difficult to comprehend by being told, correctly as far as it goes, that these are all products of evolutionary development. Our reactions to these and other natural phenomena, great and small, still hold, not in spite of, but perhaps even *because of* what we have discovered of the causes of these phenomena. There remains a mystery and a sense of wonder about both the whole that produces these reactions in us and the detail involved in such extraordinary processes. For Muslims, the God underpinning all this, both the causes of the world and our insightful awe-driven reactions to them, has neither a beginning nor an end, but is like the concept of infinity conveyed by the image of a circle. It hardly needs underlining here that many of the myths deal precisely with the wonder of the world and puzzlement at its existence and nature, puzzlement that science does nothing to diminish. Science tells us about the mechanics of the thing, but as to the genesis and endurance of those mechanics it leaves us wondering, and indeed raises the question as to why we should be constituted to wonder in this way. Religiously minded people will say that we are responding not just to something in us but also to something in or beyond the universe itself. Such thoughts should not be dismissed out of hand, nor the mythical accounts waved away as pure fantasy; there are certainly deep questions to be pondered here.

Truths about the world, then, are revealed precisely through our interactions with the world, and these will include the factual truths with which science deals, but they are by no means confined to them. The truths the romantics might have warmed to and that are referred to in the Qur'an (as we have just seen)—moral truths, human truths, truths about human potentiality and its limitations, truths about beauty and its opposite—are revealed and come alive in our dealings with the world. And I mean *truths:* notions of moral obligation, of duty, of gratitude, of beauty, of the sacred, of the principles involved in our dealings with each other, are all *truths.* They are presupposed as necessary in all our dealings in the empirical world and with each other, and are not abstracted from the empirical world in the way we might abstract the simplifications and abstractions of modern science. Nor are they, at the most basic level, constructed by us; rather, they are responses on our part to what is there, in the world, but silent and inert until we begin to act in the world, and reflect on it.

The abstractions of modern science bleach out all that we bring to the world, all that becomes alive and realized in our imaginative intercourse with the world. In the words of Douglas Hedley, "the world is neither a collection of neutral facts nor a kaleidoscope of our projected fantasies,"[8] though it can be reduced to each of these viewpoints. It is in myth above all that the mid-point in our dealings with the world between neutrality and fantasy is most powerfully evoked. And, if the world lives in us, as beings who, alone in our experience, can articulate and feel what the world is, then we ourselves will live through the meanings we find in the world. The Greek and Roman atomist myth may not be the most profound—it takes little account of our intimations of the good and the beautiful, for example, and has little of the poetry or insight or challenge we find in Pythagoras or Empedocles. But the matrix in which it is set is not that of the empiricism of modern science. Even if it is not one of the more imaginative of myths, it is one element in the classical Greek endeavor to develop a view of the world by which we might live.

This endeavor, as Popper suggested, can be seen as leading to modern science, with its literal descriptiveness, its mathematical formulae and analysis, and above all with its testability through observation and experiment. Ancient atomism may even in some forms have contained elements of what we would recognize as

---

8. Hedley, *Sacrifice Imagined*, 228.

science—a gesture toward the theoretical content of atomic science; but in itself, even if Popper is right in seeing in it some move in the direction of critical discussion, it was something far broader and more humanly resonant than what we think of today as science. The very strength of modern science arises precisely from its rigorous and exclusive attention to the empirical facts and its eschewing of human resonance. But its strength is also its weakness in its shedding of the human dimension and in its consequent and necessary blindness to our feelings and values, and more broadly in considering the way the world as a whole may generate and sustain those feelings and values.

In response to what I have just said about the necessary blindness of contemporary science to our feelings and to value, it might be said that our contemporary science is itself limited and partial, in need of drastic revision and recasting. Indeed, as we have mentioned in discussing the anthropic principle, the phenomena of consciousness and life itself, from which our feelings and sense of value arise, are themselves mysterious if we take physics, as we currently have it, to give us the form of any ultimate scientific account of these realities. This last point has been urged by a number of philosophers, materialist and non-materialist alike, who speak of the emergence of consciousness in creatures such as ourselves to be the "hard" problem, apparently immune to physicalistic explanation. How can purely physical unconscious stuff in the brain—neurons, electric charges, and the like—yield in us and other animals conscious experience, so unlike the physical stuff from which it seems to emerge?

Moreover, our sense of value, that, say, hatred or ingratitude are wrong, just wrong and not simply a reflection of our emotions, is hard to explain if it is seen as merely a byproduct of evolutionary processes; on this view, our values—including, say, our sense that genocide is just wrong—would have no objective warrant beyond contributing to the fitness of the creatures who happen to have these emotions. Maybe there could be circumstances in which genocide contributed to evolutionary fitness—and in 1881 Darwin himself looked forward to a time in which the "lower races will have been eliminated by the higher civilised races throughout the world."⁹ But surely, even if this were so, evolutionary fitness notwithstanding, it would still be wrong, just *wrong*, and hard to say otherwise when we look at the death camps and slaughter of our time. So, do we need to think in terms of a radical rethinking of our current conceptions of matter and indeed of the universe in general?

Such a thought is raised by Thomas Nagel in *Mind and Cosmos*. He writes that "an understanding of the universe as basically prone to generate life and mind will probably require a . . . radical departure from the familiar forms of naturalistic explanation. . . . Specifically in attempting to understand consciousness as a biological phenomenon, it is too easy to forget how radical is the difference between the subjective and the objective, and to fall into the error of thinking about the mental in terms taken from our ideas of physical events and processes."[10]

I have some sympathy with what Nagel says here, but he gives no sense of what this radical departure would look like or consist in. And I do not actually like the contemporary philosophical cliché, speaking of consciousness and subjectivity as being the "hard" problem or a mystery. It is not a mystery at all. All of us experience our own consciousness throughout our lives, and we are also aware that new subjects of consciousness are coming into existence every day in their hundreds of thousands. We also know how these things come about, the processes that spark off experience and life. The problem, such as it is, is that physics and science more generally, as they are today, are unable in their own terms to account for these matters of everyday experience, our own and that of the animals and living things we are surrounded with. To talk of the "hard" problem and of mysteries in this context is quite uncalled for when what should be called for is an honest recognition of the limitations of our current science.

Nevertheless, as things stand, science is as it is, and scientific explanations are as they are. And as they are, apart from coming

9. Darwin, ed., *The Life and Letters of Charles Darwin*, vol. I, 316.
10. Nagel, *Mind and Cosmos*, 127–28.

From Myth to Science

to something of a stop in dealing with conscious experience, they prescind from the view we have of the world, including our sense of value and our sense that there is meaning beyond the merely physical. If they touch on these things at all, they will tend to explain them away, as due to meaningless and value-free physical causes, and therefore strip from them their significance in our lives, in the *Lebenswelt*. An entirely new and currently unimaginable scientific perspective might change all that, but this does not alter the basic point I am making here, that science as it is does not deal with consciousness and value as they are in themselves. Its very strength actually comes precisely from its grounding in purely factual observations and evidence, from which conscious experience and all human significance is eradicated or ignored. For better or worse, this is the science admired by Popper and by so many of us for its undoubted post-Galilean achievements. Those of us who see the world as fully characterized by the theories of contemporary science all too easily see it as toneless, colorless, and de-souled, these aspects so important to our lives being dismissed as illusions or mere epiphenomena. This way of thinking about reality systematically avoids or drowns out the domain of meaning and myth, which is where the dynamic of the *Lebenswelt* would take us, if we could but hear it.

Schumann prefaced his great *Fantasie* Op 17 with a verse from Friedrich Schlegel: "Durch alle Töne tönet/ Im bunten Erdentraum/ Ein leiser Ton gezogen/ Für den, der Heimlich lautet." (Through all the tones that resound in earth's colorful dream, there sounds a faint long-drawn note for the one who listens in secret.) It is precisely the faint, long-drawn note that we find so hard to hear against the dominant materialistic worldview. But, as Schlegel says, it is there, and does make itself heard when we are confronted in our lives with what seems to be missing from that worldview. And it is particularly in opening our minds to myth, as Lewis and Tolkien recognized in their Addison's Walk conversation, that we can begin to feel the implications of the tones we might otherwise drown out.

The Prism of Truth

Although I have followed Popper in seeing much of science, ancient and modern, as being originally rooted in myth, when in the rest of this essay I talk about myth, I am intending mainly to refer to those myths that are central to a religious tradition and practice. It may be, as Pierre Hadot has urged, that the ancient Greek myths of the universe had religious overtones, concerned, as he puts it, with "a way of life and of seeing the world," concerned with "the art of living."[11] The Pythagorean and Platonic myths are certainly in a broad sense "religious." But this would not be true of some of the more modern developments in science, if, following Popper, we wanted to see them as originating from myths. The myths that will mainly concern us in what follows, as well as giving us a sense of who and where we are in the universe, will usually be embedded in a religious practice or set of such practices. Even where this embedding is not in a venerable religious tradition, as was the case with the Platonic tradition, the myths I am interested in here will presuppose and foster a religious sense, as well as exhortations as to how we should live. They will thus guide and direct their adherents as they make their journey through this life and on to what will follow after death. The questions that will concern us in the rest of this essay will be to do with the validity or truth of such overtly religious myths, how far they are mutually compatible, and where they might arise from.

---

11. Hadot, *Philosophy as a Way of Life*, 108 and 110.

5

A Storied World

MANY RELIGIOUS MYTHS OF origin have it that the world as we know it, in all its diversity and multiplicity, derives from a single unity, a One, or an ultimate supreme being of quite a different order from that of the created material world. This One, for whatever reason, creates, or has created a world apart from the original One, or is splintered into separate beings. This is often interpreted in one way or another as a "fall" on the part of the separate beings from a more perfect to a less perfect existence. The ultimate destiny of these multiple individuals is to work through this existence or life to return by some process of purification into the One or into a paradisal realm with the One, maybe after many phases of the lower form of existence, and even if that One is the "nothing" of Nirvana.

Somewhat more prosaically, but nevertheless helpfully for our purpose, we could refer here to what the seventeenth-century thinker Edward Herbert of Cherbury (incidentally the brother of the poet and divine George Herbert) referred to as "common notions."[1] These are a set of basic religious ideas that he claims are universal, in some way present in all human beings. These are:

---

1. Herbert of Cherbury, *De Veritate*, 1624 and 1645, section ix.

1) that there is a supreme Deity;

2) that this Being ought to be worshipped;

3) that virtue and piety are the chief parts of divine worship;

4) that we ought to repent of our sins and turn from them; and

5) that reward and punishment follow from the goodness and justice of God, both in this life and after.

Rather strikingly Herbert claims not just that all human beings are endowed with these common notions innately, but that different religions should be seen as different cultural expressions of them. He sees the myths underlying the different religions not so much as revelations, but rather as reminders. Even so, one could urge that the reminders have to come from somewhere, usually from a source other than the one who is being reminded. So they could still be seen as in part divinely inspired, reminders from above, so to speak.

Many of what I am calling myths can be seen as differing ways of embodying Herbert's common notions, filling them out and making them alive to the believer. Even where a myth is ostensibly silent on creation or a supreme Deity, as we saw with Buddhism and some Chinese traditions, there is still the sense that we, as individuals, are involved in a cosmic saga of purification or balance way beyond our individuality here on earth. Underlying this saga is some supra-personal force, either immanently or transcendently at work, sustaining the world as we know it. Or, given the difficulty of thinking of these things, perhaps we should think of this ultimate reality as having elements of both immanence and transcendence, but certainly transcending the world of fleeting material appearance.

As I will go on to suggest, what might be seen as the mythical or perhaps pictorial elements of the myth will point to aspects of the divine reality that are missing from Herbert's abstract characterization of the common notions, and would indeed lead me to question the apparent implication of his view, that what is really important is the Deity as abstractly characterized. These pictorial elements, or some of them, are indispensable to what the different myths are telling us and fill out the abstract common notions so as to bring us to the emotional heart of the Deity, to show it as drawing us to it. Nevertheless, Herbert's suggestion that the common notions are or may be universal, and underlying the differences between the different myths, is highly suggestive if, as I think we should, we are to see the myths as pointers to the same reality, the same ultimate Being, and as to that extent all embodying truth. But, to anticipate what will be said later, to reduce a myth to the set of abstract principles that may be discerned within it will make it a mere allegory, shorn of imaginative power. To talk in Pascalian terms, where there should be *esprit de finesse*, inspiring and talking to the whole person, the heart (Pascal's *coeur*), we will be left with *esprit de géométrie*, speaking only to our intellect (*raison*).

Let us assume that these myths—be they Vedic, Pythagorean, Platonic, Judaeo-Christian, Daoist, or whatever—have some substantial degree of truth in them. There are certainly striking family resemblances between them, along the lines just sketched, and I have no doubt that many religious or religiously charged myths that I have not mentioned share some or many of the same features, even if in somewhat different form on the surface. If they do reflect something of the ultimate reality of existence, and if the myths are widespread in various forms and long lasting, the people who developed them must have at least a partial insight into the truth or truths in question. It would not be stretching the point too far to speak of inspiration here, inspiration from above or beyond the world of everyday existence, indeed as illuminating and directing our everyday existence, and in Herbert's terms reminding us of things we may have forgotten or never knew. When we are "reminded" of these things, we may feel that at some level we knew them all the time, and in that sense are reminded (as Plato thought), but the knowledge will be buried deep within. Guesswork and fantasy may have been involved at various points in the forming and development of the myths, and in what we see ourselves as reminded of or have revealed to us through the myths, but the broad similarities between the different myths are striking.

The Prism of Truth

These striking similarities, their appearance in some form throughout most of what we know of human history, the longevity of many of them, and the way they characteristically form so substantial a part of the life, values, and ritual of the communities that embrace them, should certainly leave us open to the suggestion that what they tell us is not merely a human construction or fiction, not merely fantasy or wish fulfillment, as critics will say. Where indeed do notions of perfect divine existence and intervention in the human world come from, if not from something like a revelation, or a theophany? In what follows we will proceed on the assumption that at least some religious myths are in part revelatory of another world, revelations *from* that world. As we go, I will suggest further reasons for thinking that this might be so. But, at this point, I will simply urge that even those who would deny all possibility of any genuine revelation should be prepared to concede the value of examining the implications of thinking that there are genuine revelations from above in order to fill out just what might be involved in such a claim. This is the assumption on which I will proceed as I spell out the way in which, as I will argue, any divine revelations, if there are any such, will have to take mythical form.

In one form or another the pattern of a transcendent original unity, creation of a separate and lower world, the fall of beings into that world, accompanied by divine descent into the created world, and subsequent redemption is widespread. Even though I have expressed the pattern in Christian terms, in myths with different explicit content the essential pattern, or key aspects of it, can still be discerned. Where the myths are silent on creation, they still, as we have already said, see humanity as involved in a cosmic drama in which individuals have a need to find an orientation or balance, leading to some re-absorption into or reconciliation with the ultimate.

That myths with a similar basic structure and analogous underlying content or common notions have arisen in different places and times is itself suggestive that what those structures figure has a universal validity, as Herbert would have it. In which case they would not be merely or wholly arbitrary human constructions, much as C. S. Lewis suggested in his analysis of what he called the Tao, where there are moral truths common to all the great cultural traditions of which he was aware. (And recent anthropological studies have confirmed empirically and in some detail the correctness of Lewis's claim about the commonality of moral beliefs.)[2] Not only are these fundamental moral truths in one way or another universal (even where they sit alongside less palatable practices and beliefs, or are seen as applying only to one's own group and not to outsiders), but they are never seen by their adherents as matters of choice or human construction. When I refrain from kicking someone who is in my way, I do not think that the principle motivating this course of action is something I have constructed or something my society chose. I see the underlying principle as binding on me, from outside my (or our) menu of chosen practices. It is not like choosing to hold a fork in a certain way, or drive on the left—practices we can easily see as

---

2. See Curry, Mullins, and Whitehouse, "Is It Good to Co-operate?" The sixty societies thus studied all had some version of Lewis's Tao as central to their culture. Lewis develops his idea of the Tao in *The Abolition of Man*, 51–63. Colin Turnbull's now classic study of the Ik (*The Mountain People*) paints a picture of a tribe seemingly bereft of what we would regard as many of the most fundamental moral beliefs. However, subsequent criticism has suggested that Turnbull's own account was distorted in various ways. He overlooked aspects of Ik life that would modify his extreme claims, and also the way in which the society he was describing was in circumstances of exceptional hardship and danger, from which general conclusions about human nature should not be drawn. We might also consider at this point Ruskin's conviction that it was because of his reverent reading of the Bible in his youth that he was able later to see the depth on Homer and Horace and other "pagan" writers, leading him to "a general system of interpretation of Sacred literature,—both classical and Christian," which would enable one "to sympathise with the faiths of candid and generous souls, of every age and every clime." And he goes on to ask who built Amiens Cathedral, this "Parthenon of Gothic architecture," and answers: "God and Man—is the first and most true answer. The stars in their courses built it, and the Nations. Greek Athena labours here, and Roman Father Jove and Guardian Mars. The Gaul labours here, and the Frank, knightly Norman— mighty Ostrogoth, and wasted anchorite of Idumea." In other words, continuity between Christian and classical, not just in religion, but also in forms of art and architecture. (From *The Bible of Amiens* [1885], ch. 3, section 52, and ch. 4, sections 11 and 12.)

alterable, a matter of choice, collective or personal. Fundamental moral principles do not impinge on us as matters of human choice, even where philosophical analysts, such as Sartre or Rorty, who deny any basic human essence, will tell us that they are. Phenomenologically that is not how moral obligation presents itself to us and works on us.

If C. S. Lewis was moved by the myths of Balder, Adonis, and Bacchus, and if we are tantalized by the Enuma Elish, this cannot be because of the surface details, which, looked at purely scientifically or even historically are just too bizarre to merit examination (as we can see from the unimaginative and remorselessly literalist incursion into this area by the likes of Richard Dawkins and Daniel Dennett). It must be because through those details, and infusing those details with significance, we feel, feel with a steadfast heart, that something of deep importance about our life, and beyond our life, is being awakened within us through the mythical narrative. So long as we stay on the scientific-empirical level, the level of Pascal's intellect or *raison*, no such feelings or sensitivity will be awakened.

Science is just one damn thing after another, with no message above or beyond, and no more significance to one event or action than to any other, not even to our own lives or to the lives of those dear to us. And even history, in its classic foundational "Was ist eigentlich geschehen?" mode—what actually happened?—can give us no sense of the *meaning* of those happenings for us *now*. When we hear a myth, especially a powerful and resonant one, other vistas are opened, vistas to which we respond, which involve us and speak directly to us, and which, even if we cannot say exactly why, open new levels of being and feeling to us. Of course, if no one responded in this way to a given myth, it would not have any significance, and would be no more than a fantasy of brief duration. But this was clearly not the case with the myths that entranced C. S. Lewis, even before his conversion, nor is it the case with many, many people when confronted with the ancient religious myths embedded in their culture, and to which they respond in the depths of their being.

Indeed, given that we as human beings are always prone to look beyond the merely factual or scientific, but to see the world and our own existence in terms of meanings that explain why and for what purpose things are as they are, it is entirely to be expected that we will have a predilection for myths, for narratives that give meaning to the world as it is, and that explain origins and destinies. One could at this point ask why it is that we do have this predilection, this sense that there is something higher, and quest for it. Is this predilection simply an epiphenomenal byproduct of the musings of meaningless particles and lumps of matter (us)? Or are we and our consciousness constituted in such a way as to be open to revelations about our ultimate destiny, and, as Augustine said long ago, to be restless until we find our true home in a realm beyond the universe?

We suggested in connection with the anthropic principle that the potential for consciousness had to be present in the universe from the beginning. Consciousness, or perhaps better self-consciousness, in our case—a questioning of the things we are conscious of—is inclined to reject the notion that existence is meaningless. Our self-consciousness also has within it intimations of perfection, a sense of what would be ultimately be fitting. This inborn sense of the ultimately fitting responds to mythical meanings, which take the form of stories about the meaning of the universe in general, and of our lives in particular. Given the manner in which all our capacities, including this responsiveness to myth, are embryonically present from the beginning of time (or always, if we think the universe is eternal), it could be said that the universe in which we live is at all times, and long before our appearance in it, a "storied" world (to use a phrase of Mark Wynn). The meaning of existence in that universe is given in stories. The universe is one from which stories and myths are prone to emerge from those who live within and through and by it. We, in a sense, tell the story, or some of the stories, that the world itself exists to have told.

Or, as we have already seen in Rilke's *Ninth Duino Elegy*, we are here to make the inarticulate earth articulate, in his own words, to "resurrect in ourselves [the earth] invisibly. Is not your dream one day to be invisible"—through our perceptions, our words, our art, our poetry, to express what the world and nature are. We are thus, as Rilke says in his famous letter of November 13, 1925, to Witold von Hulewicz, "bees of the invisible, passionately collecting the honey of the invisible, storing it in the great golden hive of the invisible." We thus transform what is dumb and transient and visible in its brute materiality into eloquent and enduring value and meaning. This is the role that has been accorded to us since the beginning. In fulfilling this role, we transpose the sheer materiality of what confronts us in the world to products of human consciousness, stories, images, poetry, music, and the like.

It would take us too far afield at this point to go into detail here, but it is surely significant that we in the materialistic West have for some time tended to live in a culture in which there is no prevailing myth to structure and accord our lives meaning. Consequently, our lives, private and public, have come to seem increasingly disjointed and meaningless, under political dispensations of both left and right. As Erich Heller argued in *The Disinherited Mind*, poets and artists of the twentieth century and subsequently, such as Rilke and Yeats, have been increasingly drawn to constructing their own ever more personal and idiosyncratic mythologies. As he put it:

> Without that all-pervasive sense of truth which bestows on happier cultures their intuition of order and reality, poetry—in company with all the other arts—will be faced with ever increasing demands for ever greater "creativeness." For the "real order" has to be "created" where there is no intuitive conviction that it exists.... In the great poetry of the European tradition the emotions do not interpret; they respond to the interpreted world.[3]

The interpretation to which they responded was given by and structured through the mythology of the time, the Christianity that, for all its faults, was pervasive for well over a millennium and a half.

---

3. Heller, *The Disinherited Mind*, 170–72.

A further sign of this disinheritance is that in the visual arts up to the Baroque era and even beyond, paintings had a wealth of religious and mythological meaning, which had to be understood to appreciate the full significance of the artist's intentions, whereas you need to know nothing beyond what is immediately apparent in the image to appreciate impressionist and most twentieth-century art. Heller goes on to suggest that with ever greater poetic hermeticism, the world itself becomes ever more impoverished. It is just the situation we are in today when factual discourse of the scientific sort, as we saw in discussing Wittgenstein earlier, becomes all that can be significantly or seriously said.

Of course, having a truth-revealing religious myth to structure one's life does not mean that one's behavior is necessarily any better. But, as we see in looking at the history of the Middle Ages in Europe, even the most cruel and unscrupulous of rulers understood that their behavior was wicked and would be judged. According to Dante, Manfred, a brutally proud and religiously excommunicated medieval warrior, begged for divine forgiveness as he was dying in battle. So he is in purgatory rather than in hell, where his bloody deeds would otherwise have sent him, and where he is worried that his daughter might believe him to be (and so not see any point in praying for his soul) (*Purgatorio*, III, 110ff.). What is striking about this passage is not so much Dante's invention, as the fact that Dante and his contemporary readers could naturally think that the deeds of a Manfred could send him to everlasting punishment. And also that the deeds even of a man of such pride and heartlessness could at the last moment be redeemed by divine grace.

As we have already stated, philosophically speaking, if we want to speak of God, or of the One, we have to envisage this ultimate Being as beyond our powers of comprehension and of language. Our understanding of the divine therefore has to be metaphorical or analogical, so it is entirely to be expected that there will be different ways of approaching that reality in different cultures and at different times. Moreover, when our understanding of the divine is presented in mythical form, through a myth, the myth will characteristically be open-ended, an example of something possessing Keats's negative capability, leaving us "capable of being in uncertainties, mysteries, doubts, without any irritable reaching after fact and reason."[4]

Myths of this sort will not be allegories, in which there is a one-to-one correspondence between a figure in the allegory and the reality or person allegorized, but open-ended in their implications, intimating a multitude of further interpretations and shades of meaning. It is not that we wouldn't or shouldn't probe these further implications and intimations, but the spirit in which we do this should itself be open-ended, exploratory, not attempting to close the thing off with irritable dogmatism. With a myth, it is often the case that it is only after living with it for some time that one sees that the words one thinks one is familiar with really mean more than one ever imagined or could articulate literally. C. S. Lewis goes further, suggesting that we can feel myths "to be numinous. It is as if something of great moment has been communicated to us. The recurrent efforts of the mind to grasp—we mean, chiefly, to conceptualise—this something, are seen in the persistent tendency of humanity to provide myths with allegorical explanations. And after all allegories have been tried, the myth itself continues to feel more important than they."[5]

Perhaps strangely in the light of this eloquent statement of the difference between myth and allegory, Tolkien criticized Lewis's own Narnia myth as being too close to allegory, too tightly constrained by the lineaments of Christian doctrine, so that we can read off figures in the tale as representing this or that Christian persona or reality. It is as if Lewis already had in mind Christ, let us say, when developing this character, the devil and the disciples when drawing others, and so on. Fair or not as a criticism of Lewis, we can see the point of the criticism, a criticism that would not apply to Tolkien's own much more diffuse and self-generating mythologizing, or indeed to what Lewis himself saw as the strength of myth. The persons and realities in myths are what Coleridge

---

4. John Keats, letter to his brothers, December 22, 1817.
5. Lewis, *An Experiment in Criticism*, 44.

called "tautegorical." That is to say, they stand for themselves and not, as in allegory, for something else, but what they stand for goes beyond their surface appearance and meaning. Coleridge here follows Schlegel, for whom an allegorical image acts as a concept that completely captures the thing being allegorized, whereas a symbol is an idea, something with its own life and resonance, going beyond the comparison intended in the symbol, and in itself not fully capturable. The thought is well expressed in one of Goethe's *Aphorisms on Art and Art History*: "Symbolism transforms the appearance into an idea, the idea into an image, and in such a way that the idea remains infinitely powerful and unattainable in the image, and even if expressed in every language would remain unattainable."[6]

More prosaically perhaps than Goethe and Schlegel, but with analytical clarity, we also have Peter Winch pointing out that a "picture can be an essential aspect of a form of representation without itself *constituting* the representation."[7] Helpfully from our point of view, he goes on to give the example of a woman who has just lost her son in a terrible accident, and believes that she will be reunited with him in death—but without thinking of this reunion as analogous to a reunion in life, or indeed being able to say what exactly this will amount to. Nevertheless, this firm but not irrational belief inspires and consoles. This is helpful, because it suggests once more that when we are thinking of mythical pictures of religious matters, we should not think of the myths as giving us scientific or historical pictures of what it is they are referring to. They are, as we are arguing, mythical representations, essential to the thought, as Winch insists, but not to be looked at as literal representations, or even in the narrow sense allegorical.

Thus symbols, or more precisely the use of symbols in myth, will be particularly appropriate when we reach out to the ungraspable divine. Through their deployment of natural forms, myths enable us to see intimations of transcendence arising from and

---

6. Goethe, "Aphorisms on Art and Art History," 229. On Coleridge and the tautegorical, see Hedley, *Coleridge, Philosophy and Religion*, 133–36.

7. Winch, "Picture and Representation," 10.

within the everyday, the divine in the natural. And so the notion of incarnation is very much as home in myths. It is obviously crucial in the Christian myth and central to it, though not unique to it. Myths, whether explicitly incarnatory or not, are, as Jadwiga Swiatecka has memorably put it, "visual tips of an ontological iceberg."[8]

Following on from Swiatecka, Roger Scruton somewhat enigmatically speaks of the biblical account of creation and the fall as a myth of origin, a fiction, but one illustrating a deep truth: "It purports to be an account of what actually happened, in those six days of creation. It speaks of an original union of man and God, sundered by the free actions of our 'first parents,' after which mankind wandered the world in conflict and desolation. And the New Testament offers a final redemption, one already foretold by the prophets. The price of that original sin has now been paid by God himself, and the way back to oneness with God at last lies open to us."[9] And he goes on to point out that many ancient religions have a similar structure, such as the cults of Isis and Osiris, Attis and Adonis, to say nothing of the Catholic sacrament of penance and Greek tragedies, such as those of the *Oresteia* and Oedipus. The deep truth(s) Scruton discerns in these myths are beneath the fictional garment, or are the ontological icebergs beneath what we see on the surface of the sea. But, for those who see value in the myths, what they tell us about human life and, I would add, about our relation to the divine is not to be seen as fictional (and here I may go beyond what Scruton himself is prepared to accept). If there is truth in the myths, and I want to say that there is, then we must surely construe that truth as not just about terrestrial human life. It will also take us into our relationship with God, or however we are conceiving the ultimate Being.

To speak in unforgivably anthropomorphic terms, given that all human attempts to understand the divine are bound to be partial and incomplete, this will naturally suggest a picture of God revealing Godself in different ways to different groups. As argued

---

8. Swiatecka, *The Idea of the Symbol*, 59.
9. Scruton, *The Soul of the World*, 108–9.

A Storied World

earlier, even if we are agnostic on God and divine revelation, there is some point in thinking of these myths of origin and of redemption as having more than a metaphorical validity, as being more than fantasies of deliverance, in analyzing just what such a claim would entail. We should, at least for the sake of argument, not see them as purely human creations. We should be willing to entertain the idea that they are what they say they are, revelations from a higher source, so as to see what such an idea would imply.

But I would want to urge that we do more than simply consider the implication of claiming that such and such a myth is a divine revelation. I think that there are strong reasons for thinking that some myths may actually be divine revelations. Critics will insist at this point that their transcendent claims and conceptions are purely a matter of wish fulfillment on the part of those who hold to them. But such myths are found in pretty well all human cultures of which we are aware. Myths of a purportedly divine provenance are humanly pervasive. There is also deep wisdom contained in very many of them (admittedly often with distortions too). All this suggests strongly that they may actually be what they all say or imply they are, namely, revelations from beyond the purely human. Their universality and the strength these myths have on the millions who hold to them surely requires a stronger explanation of their source than the somewhat empty idea that all they amount to is wish fulfillment. If that were all they are, wouldn't they long ago have died out? We have indeed plenty of examples of particular forms of these myths dying away, and also of some of the more frankly bizarre or incredible aspects of them, but in transformed or new forms their essence lives on in human minds and hearts.

In view of their strength, persistence, and indeed (with qualifications) their wisdom, I would urge that we actually do more than simply entertain the possibility of their divine source and actually think of them as in part inspired from above, as divine self-revelations, as theophanies, as outward movements of divine self-revelation, but as refracted through the human minds receiving them. Where do these notions come from? What explains their hold on us? How is it they are so pervasive and lapidary, in contrast to the way mere fantasy, fairy stories, and Santa Claus are not? In what follows, and whether my readers will go along with my own position or not, I am now going to work on the basis that the major religious myths are, at least in part, what they imply they are. I hope, though, that even those who would not be prepared to follow me in seeing religious myths, or some of them, as divinely inspired will see the point of working on the assumption that they are, to see just what is involved in such a claim.

These human minds, which articulate the revelations for us, will preeminently include those who in their traditions are known as prophets, those seen as charged with conveying messages from the divine to the human, often in states of mystical and visionary transport. They are then, as Muhammad was, seen by the followers who collect around them as inspired, as being the medium through which a more-than-human wisdom is transmitted. Strikingly, this wisdom often castigates the community and individuals for their failings, but also contains a promise of redemption or salvation for those who mend their ways. Do we have to see different messengers from different traditions as necessarily conflicting, or could they be at a deep level in harmony with each other?

On the mutual complementarity of different messengers or prophets, Ruskin is evocative, revealing, and tantalizingly evasive:

> And I call it a magnificent principle, for it is an eternal and universal one, not in art only, but in human life. It is the great principle of Brotherhood, not by quality, not by likeness, but by giving and receiving, that souls that are unlike, and natures that are unlike, by being bound into one noble whole by each receiving something from and of the others' gifts and the others' glory . . . in whatever has been made by the Deity externally delightful to the human sense of beauty, there is some type of God's nature, or of God's law; nor are any of His laws . . . greater than the appointment that the most lovely and perfect unity shall be obtained by the taking of one nature into another. . . .[10]

---

10. Ruskin, *Stones of Venice*, 24.

A Storied World

The passage is from volume III of *The Stones of Venice*—magnificently appropriate to our theme, given that Venice stood at the crossroads of Catholic Europe, Greek Byzantium, and the Muslim Ottoman Empire, and even dealing in the trade of luxuries from the Far East; and uniting all these influences "in its lovely and perfect *unity*." Does Ruskin overstate things here and compress his own intuition, almost squeezing the life out of it? Should he, and we, stress rather the way that "souls that are unlike" and "natures that are unlike" can all live together by giving, receiving, and returning, and yet maintaining their own essence, without being compressed into an overpowering and life-squeezing unity. That, I think, would be the better way of looking at the interaction between different theophanies, enriching each other, speaking to each other, but without ever collapsing into each other. After all, even a synthetic unity of all the myths we have would still be incomplete as a representation of the divine. Any such representation, including one that seems to bring things together, absolutely needs difference and tension with others to avoid collapsing into a presumptuous misrepresentation of the way the Divine must forever elude even the best and most inspired of our attempts to capture it in our terms. So, while seeing God's nature in each appeal to our sense—perhaps better, *senses*—of beauty, the giving and receiving and returning must lead to a one noble whole, but a whole that still admits difference and even tension within.

So, given that no human understanding in this domain can be complete, a diversity of approaches to the ultimate can also have its advantages, in showing different perspectives on it, and also in cautioning those with one particular version of the truth from insisting that they and they alone have *the* truth. Every source of truth is unavoidably a source of falsehood, as Peter Hacker warned us, and the particular form of falsehood to which myth is prone is that of a cold-hearted, bureaucratic dogmatism, with the imaginative, open-ended dimension of the myth strangled and squeezed out. The myth will be reduced to a tightly structured allegory, stripped of its endlessly interpretive potential. And worse, doing this will lead to intolerance, persecution, and worse. As Ruskin puts it, "the greater part of the sins of the Church have been brought on it by enthusiasm, which in passionate contemplation and advocacy of parts of Scripture, easily grasped, neglected the study and at last betrayed the balance of the rest."[11] In the literalism of the enthusiasts, the myth will become a dead thing, to "man's destruction," as Ruskin says. It will become a carcass of desiccated fact and bullying reason, over which fanatical scholars and religious officials fight it out, and too often in the process even kill each other, as well as the myth itself.

---

11. Ruskin, *The Bible of Amiens*, 111.

6

A Plenitude of Myths

IT IS IN THE modern world that we have become acutely conscious of the existence of different religious and mythical traditions in the world, and also more aware of the problems this brings for those asserting the uniqueness of their myth. Does this mean that those from other traditions are deprived of a route to the divine, of redemption, if we put it in those terms? Or that in the terms of *our* myth, *our* religion, those outside our religious community cannot be saved? Some have thought so, *extra ecclesiam nulla salus* (no salvation outside the church) being a chilling and hectoring thought, embraced even by Dante with his First Circle of virtuous pagans, living eternally "without hope or desire" (*Inferno* IV, 42).

Some recent theologians have tried to mollify this censoriousness by talk of "anonymous Christians," people who lived before Christ or those living since his death who had never heard of him, but who have lived lives of Christian virtue. However, David Jones's Romano-British Arthurian priest in *The Sleeping Lord* is more generous, more humane, more Christian, and more aware of true transcendence: he prays for all the dead of the whole world, from all the past millennia right back to the unknown beginnings of human life. In the Mass he remembers these all, as Jones puts it, quietly and silently making on their behalf the sign of salvation and speaking the liturgical words "Requiem aeternam dona eis, Domine" (Grant them eternal rest, O Lord).[1] *Eis*—for these *all*, and not just for the marked elect of an exclusionary church or sect, or those "generously" permitted an anonymous membership. David Jones thus shows the Christian myth capable of meeting and encompassing the followers of all the others, without need for apology or prevaricating explanation.

The exclusivist position David Jones is rejecting is not just unappealing from a moral and ethical point of view. It also accords to our own myth, if we are Christian, a uniquely privileged role it cannot have. If all religions and all religious myths point to a reality that is inherently beyond what any human speech can tell us, as Aquinas suggests in his insistence on the need for analogical speech here, words with a sense beyond their literal meaning, then no one myth can say *all* that there is to be said, or indeed say *any* of it with literal exactitude. Moreover, each myth and each tradition has its own particularity, its own way of conceiving the universal ultimate.

Yet even as the particularity of a myth becomes more delineated, its adherents will assert its claims to be true. Logically and humanly the very act of asserting something implies a claim to a universally acceptability. Assertion in itself implies that anyone who considers the matter will also be able to discern that it is as I am asserting it to be. So asserting anything, including the tenets of a preferred religious myth, opens the tenets of what I am saying up to the claims of competing systems, even if its adherents may not be willing to recognize this. Assertion itself, whether of bare fact or religious system, presupposes a universal acceptability and rationality to which it aims, as at least a regulative principle. So, in asserting something, I open up what I say to dialogue and discussion with those inhabiting contrasting systems and competing views, and maybe to correction from them.[2]

---

1. Jones, *The Sleeping Lord and Other Fragments*, 86.

2. On this point, and related issues, I have benefited from conversations with Alan Montefiore and Perry Marshall, and from Montefiore's *Philosophy and the Human Paradox*.

A Plenitude of Myths

A relevant example here would be when a critic of literalistic biblical Christianity points out some of the many problems involved in conceiving of creation as taking place over *six* days, over days that apparently can be measured before the creation of the sun on the fourth day, to say nothing of there being light and vegetation on earth before the creation of the sun. Sensible believers, sensitive to the norms of reasonable belief and discourse will, of course, quite reasonably reply that the book of Genesis should not be understood as a literal historic and scientific account of creation, but in quite a different way, to underline the majesty and power as well as the care and concern of the creator, something that goes beyond any factual or scientific account.

Biblical interpretation aside, our very conception of the transcendent must lay us open to the possibility of contrasting mythological expressions of that reality, each with its own distinctive emphasis and way of approaching the goal. For Menachem Fisch, this applies especially in areas of scientific theory and moral and political principles, as well as, needless to say here, in religious and theological matters. In all these cases Fisch, following Popper, sees the need for a critical approach (and he finds a similar view somewhat obliquely expressed in Ecclesiastes). But, so long as we remain within our own perspective, any criticisms we make will be severely limited and curtailed at the often-unspoken foundations of our thinking. To achieve a genuinely critical approach to what we believe we will actually have to face and consider alternative perspectives to our own openly and honestly, so as to resolve some of the narrowness and unrealized prejudice in our own. This going beyond our own perspective and seeking enlightenment from other traditions will be particularly necessary in thinking of a transcendent ultimate, which, as we have seen, necessarily eludes full human understanding.[3] Indeed, an adherent to a particular myth, realizing the necessary limitations of his or her myth, should actually be open to the possibility of insights he or she had not contemplated from his or her perspective. He or she should look

---

3. Fisch and Band, *Qohelet: Searching for a World Worth Living*, esp. pp. 3–6 and 136–39.

with favor on aspects of other myths, were these brought to his or her attention, even seek them out in a spirit of honest cooperation in what is bound to be an unending quest. But even while having universal acceptability and critico-collaborative conversation as a regulative ideal, we should still see particular myths as potentially and at time actually having a partial grasp of metaphysical, ultimate truth. We should cherish these distinctive ways, and our own in particular, as pointers to the transcendent. We should see them as imaginative intimations of the divine, as perspectives that may have a limited validity, but a validity nonetheless, and thus as giving us directions in which our thoughts and feelings might tend. As Dante suggested with his vision of a human face in and behind the mysterious Trinity in the final canto of *Paradiso*, something profound can be conveyed even in an impossible image. To put this point another way, the impossible image might be striving to represent contraries that can be reconciled, but that are encompassed in reality in ways hard for us to comprehend so long as we remain on the descriptive-factual level.

Emphasizing both the transcendent and the figurative sides of myths of the divine, the early sixteenth-century theologian and Roman cardinal Egidio de Viterbo has it that, "as Dionysius says, the divine ray cannot reach us unless it is covered by poetic veils."[4] No doubt, unless it were so covered, its very strength and brilliance would blind us, and certainly crush any freedom we had. "Ubi summa lux, tibi summa tenbrae; ubi summa quoque tenebrae, ibi summum lumen" (where there is the greatest light, there to you is the greatest darkness; but where there is the greatest darkness, there is also the greatest light), a saying of Marsilio Ficino, to whom we will shortly turn.

From a different, but nonetheless mythically inspired source, when Goethe's Faust awakens to a new life at the start of the mythologically suffused second part of the drama, he says "Am farbigen Abglanz haben wir das Leben" (in a coloured, pale reflection do we have our life). The context is the rising of the sun when Faust awakens to start his post-Gretchen adventures, a life-awakening burst

---

4. Quoted by Edgar Wind, in *Pagan Mysteries in the Renaissance*, 25.

of the sun, but, like Plato's sun in the myth of the cave, blinding and overpowering. Faust has to turn his back on the sun itself, but then he sees the magnificent waterfalls cascading down the rocks surrounding him, and he also sees the colored rainbow reflections of the sun's light in the ever-pouring streams. In a reflection of the full reality, yes, but pale as it is in comparison to the full reality, this vibrant, fascinating reflection is the best we can hope for, and in its way good enough, when not distracted by care, want, need, and desire, as Faust increasingly became.

Another way of bringing out the conception of religious myth I am here developing would be to refer to what Edmund Burke perceptively wrote about the fundamental truths of morality, which must underlie any acceptable political arrangement. These fundamental truths, which are necessary to structure a decent way of living, will be diffused throughout human history in different and at times even apparently conflicting ways. What Burke calls these "metaphysic rights" (somewhat analogous to C. S. Lewis's Tao) enter into our "common life like rays of light which pierce into a dense medium, [and which] are, by the laws of nature, refracted from their straight line. Indeed in the gross and complicated mass of human passions and concerns, the primitive rights of men undergo such a variety of refractions and reflections, that it becomes absurd to talk of them as if they continued in the simplicity of their original direction."[5] So it will be with religious light or inspiration, as it enters the human world in mythologized form. For better and also for worse this light will be refracted and reflected through human concerns and passions. But, for better or worse, we should respect the forms in which the light reaches us. As Tolkien once observed of the attempt to uncover the pure meaning of the gospel behind the ways its message has come down to us through the doctrines and traditions of the church (or churches), in attempting to retrieve the sapling from inside the oak, we will end up by destroying both.

We should be careful of losing the insights evoked in the great religious myths in our attempts to rationalize and sanitize them.

---

5. Burke, *Reflections on the Revolution in France*, 152.

So, as I qualified Herbert of Cherbury's reduction of myth to his abstract common notions, I am wary of following John Hick when he argued that we should seek something *behind* all the myths. For Hick, this would be "an ultimate ground of the intentional objects of the different forms of religious thought and experience," a Real that cannot be said to be "one or many, person or thing, substance or process, good or evil, purposive or non-purposive." Not good or evil, not purposive or non-purposive, in no sense personal, not even one? Some definite and positive claims from each of these contraries can surely be elicited, and rightly elicited, from the great religious traditions that have captivated our species. And to take something positive and veridical from a myth or set of myths means that we must reject Hick's own attempt to see the great religious myths as in no sense true, as, in his words, "manifestly inadequate." He says that we should not attempt to see them as possessing more than what he calls a practical truthfulness. That is, we should see them simply as directions as to the conduct of our own lives, and not as anything descriptively true, or even suggestive of truth about the divine or what he calls the Real, though even practical truthfulness must be problematic if the Real to which they point is as unspecified as Hick has it.[6]

Indeed, were a myth to appear to promulgate evil or inhumanity, we would be inclined to reject it as authoritative, and maybe to regard it, or at least the offending part of it, as a piece of self-deceptive perversity and self-dramatization on the part of its adherents, along the lines of some piece of late nineteenth-century decadence, a *nostalgie de la boue*. This is because we are first and foremost human beings, endowed with a moral sense, which colors our reaction to what we hear and what we are taught. We are, as it were, pre-programmed with the Tao, as we have seen C. S. Lewis claiming. This pre-programming we bring to the myths we encounter. If not perverse, and to the extent they are not perverse,

---

6. Hick, *An Interpretation of Religion*, 350 and 246. My disagreement with Hick notwithstanding, at many points his detailed analyses of the great religious myths and their similarities and differences are revealing. In general, though, he stresses the differences between the myths where I would see underlying continuities.

A Plenitude of Myths

these myths will in their turn embody something like Lewis's Tao or aspects of it, reinforcing the same moral sense. So it is no coincidence that the powerful myths that have captivated human kind in a deep religious sense, and about which Hick writes, seem in different ways to agree on fundamental virtues and vices. Limitations notwithstanding, they all seem to point to a basic structure of reality, similar at core points, in one way or another embodying the same common notions, but also different, and suggestively different, in emphasis, imagery, and articulation. In these powerful myths, we find the antithesis of nothingness, disorder, rigidity, and injustice, together with a sense of our own lives being grounded in a Reality that is itself groundless and, in the last resort, incomprehensible to us.[7] Geoffrey Hill's powerful words about "knowledge granted at the final withholding" are relevant here, or should it be knowledge withheld at the final illumination?[8]

Having just criticized Hick, he is helpful and illuminating on the common core of the religious myths we would be disposed to find acceptable: "Love, compassion, self-sacrificing concern for the good of others, generous kindness and forgiveness" are not, he says, alien ideas imposed by supernatural authority, but arise out

---

7. Regarding the basic structure of reality as understood by the major religious faiths, while this is not the place to discuss Buddhism in any detail, we should underline that the "nothingness" that is gestured at in the Buddhist scriptures is very far from a nihilistic or destructive or atheistic nothingness; in the light of the Buddha's own apparent refusal to define what is to be believed in this area, it could perhaps be seen as a way of intimating a plenitude that surpasses understanding and categorization. There is certainly a notion of ultimate truth and serenity or nirvana (even if nirvana is seen as cessation of rebirth, is it actually *total* nothingness?). It is no doubt significant that the ostensibly atheistic basis of early Buddhism quite easily developed into the far more metaphysically absolutist tradition of the Mahayana schools. One might also offer the caste system in India as a counterexample to the proposal that religions share fundamental virtues and vices. However, as far as the Hindu case of Untouchables (Dalits) goes, as many commentators aver, should this not be treated as a relatively late deformation of the main thrust of the spirituality in the Vedas and in Hinduism more generally? Similar considerations could apply to the treatment meted out by many Christians in history to Jews, Muslims, and even to other Christians on the "wrong" side of a doctrinal line.

8. Hill, *The Orchards of Syon*, Canto XX, p. 20.

of our human nature (as with Lewis's Tao), and are "reinforced, refined and elevated to new levels within the religious traditions." (New levels, we might add, as part of a revelation from above, even if anticipated in our human nature.) And he goes on to suggest that if Gautama had preached an Eightfold Path of selfishness, greed, hatred, and violence, if Christ had extolled hatred rather than love, or if Muhammad had not embodied in his own life submission to God, then none of these men would have been regarded as true prophets. And in the light of this basic understanding of human nature embodied in the great religious traditions, we can judge other purported revelations, and also lament where the traditions we might favor have themselves fallen short (caste outcasts and the burning of brides in Hinduism, Muslim persecution of Bahá'ís and others, Hindu-Sikh violence in India, Catholic-Protestant bigotry and worse in Ireland, and so on, and unfortunately so on, things that still go on, even after all the evil in past religious history).[9] So our basic moral sense does give us a basis on which to judge and value religious traditions and also to criticize even the ones whose foundation and essence we might cherish.

However, rather than seeking to brush away the mythological content of all religions in favor of a universal *via negativa*, in which we are left with an entirely empty, contentless conception of the Real, we should see that each of the conceptions of the divine in the various myths before us may, imaginatively, give genuine insight into the nature of the divine, insights that push mainly in the same direction in each of the dilemmas proposed by Hick, namely, in the "common notion" direction. In his short essay "Myth Becomes Fact" C. S. Lewis emphasizes both the plurality and the parallelisms between different myths, as well as their intrinsic value: "We must not be nervous about 'parallels' and 'pagan myths': they ought to be there—it would be a stumbling block if they weren't. We must not, in false spirituality, withhold our imaginative welcome. If God chooses to be mythopoeic—and is not the sky itself a myth?—shall we refuse to be mythopathic."[10] Perhaps going

---

9. Cf. Hick, *An Interpretation of Religion*, 325–27.
10. Lewis, "God in the Dock," 67.

beyond Lewis here, we would suggest that it is not just that God *chooses* to be mythopoeic: given the nature of our sensibility and the utter transcendence of the divine, it is that our route to God can *only* by mythic.

We could extend the Thomistic line on analogy at this point. Aquinas tells us that in referring to the divine we have to use our (human) words analogically, that is, as having a sense beyond the literal. The same might be said of the mythological structures through which the divine is represented to us. They too are to be seen in analogical terms, as pointing to the truth, but to a truth that is always more than the pictures in which we are able to conceive it, and beyond any and all of them in ways we (like Dante) are unable fully to grasp. We should not treat our own myth as if it is a scientific or photographic representation of the divine.

There could not, for example, be a photograph of Christ's ascension, the mere thought of which would lead, if not to absurdity, at least to pointless and insoluble speculation about what happened to Christ's body: once it had disappeared from sight in a cloud, how could a physical human body then get transformed into a different state of being altogether and continue into heaven? Equally, while we could photograph Christ's crucifixion, we could not show how he was the Son of God. (Dostoyevsky supposedly disliked Holbein's realistic painting of *The Body of the Dead Christ* [1520–22] precisely because it made the Son of God look like just a corpse; but what else could it do? Are the Orthodox icons with which Dostoyevsky was familiar more true to the Christian myth because they suggest something elevatedly supernatural, unharmed even, in representing the Pietà?)

Both Christ's incarnation and ascension will be seen by the Christian as revealing truths about Christ's nature and salvific mission, truths that are in our terms mythological rather than factual in a scientific sense. Certainly, they are not events that could be impartially recorded under those descriptions by a camera clicking or whirring away at the relevant time. If there was anything to be seen, it would be something that would not look like how the event is seen by believers, something that on the face of it would be perfectly mundane, perfectly factual in the terms we are thinking of facts.

Michelangelo, *The Creation of Adam* (1508–12)

In a striking comment on Michelangelo's *Creation of Adam*, D. Z. Phillips says that God is in the picture, creating and self-emptying, but does not enter it as a picture, as pictured, we might say. The picture is not representational. The creation of Adam was not like that; God is not like that. But for those who can see it for what it is, Michelangelo's image, with its incredible power, will convey a deep truth about the divine self-emptying of the creation, with Adam's own nakedness conveying his own existence as unencumbered by the vain apparels of this world.[11] I suspect that not even the most hardened atheist will, despite his or her unbelief, fail to grasp something of what Michelangelo is getting at, which, no more than the book of Genesis itself, is to be understood literally or factually.

Apropos of Michelangelo's *Creation of Adam*, no one will need reminding that the creator is depicted as a magnificently virile, mature, even elderly man, a patriarch indeed. But without getting involved in tiresome controversies about the language of the liturgy—God as "he," "him," etc.—it is surely worth pointing out

11. Phillips, "Pictures of Eternity," 77.

that to balance the force and strength involved in creation, there is an equally forceful femininity involved, creation as having womb-like and maternal aspects. This is surely recognized in ancient Greek mythology, where along with the sky-bound and procreatively powerful Ouranos, there is also Gaia, the earth itself as mother and source of life in its teeming and inter-connected fruitfulness. We could also point here to the wisdom tradition in the biblical book of Proverbs, where God creates the cosmos through Wisdom, and the divine Wisdom is envisaged as a female figure, even as like a goddess who was "set up from everlasting, from the beginning" (8:23, see also 3:15–21). It seems that these passages formed the basis of a whole Jewish tradition of divine Wisdom, or Sophia, which of course has its resonance in Christianity, particularly in the Orthodox tradition.

Sandro Botticelli, *The Birth of Venus* (1484–86)

We could also remember that Venus or Aphrodite, sensual *and* divine love in Botticelli's unforgettable image, arises from a sea fructified by the seed of the castrated Uranus or Ouranos and is then clothed in the vesture of spring, a myth Plato in the *Republic* (378a) would rather we forgot, but somewhat narrow-mindedly so, once we understand its resonance. Both feminine and masculine poles are aspects of the transcendent creative force we, as humans, try to capture in our myths, focusing at one time on one aspect and at another on the other. But we should not think of the transcendent in terms of any simple bi-polarity. There is also the creative fire, so central to Zoroastrianism, but also in Heraclitus, the ever-changing, ever-living fire in and behind all things. This fire throbs and pulses even in what appears to us to be the most solid and impermeable rocks. Nature is, as Hopkins puts it, Heraclitean fire. Of course, Ouranos, Gaia and the Heraclitean fire cannot all be coherently captured in one image or discursive account, which is partly why I am emphasizing the need for several and mutually contrasting (though not contradicting) myths when we approach the transcendent.

A further hint as to how myths are to be looked at is given by some artistic representations of divine visions, in which the visionary is seen as seeing something, a divine figure, for example, which bystanders cannot see. Striking examples of this approach are the paintings of Paul's conversion on the road to Damascus by both Michelangelo and Caravaggio.

Michelangelo, *The Conversion of Saul* (c. 1542–45)

A Plenitude of Myths

Caravaggio, *The Conversion of Saint Paul* (1600)

All that the other figures in the paintings see is Saul on the ground, but they are unaware of what is going on for Saul himself. They do not see what we as readers of the book of Acts see, *why* he is fallen and dumb. Although in the Michelangelo the visionary content is shown in the picture, it is shown as something not publicly or photographically available, which may be a helpful way of looking at the manner in which the meaning of myths does not reside in their literal content. The meaning resides in that part of their content that, as in the case of the birth of Christ, say, goes beyond the empirical or factual basis of the myth.

Raphael, *Ezekiel's Vision* (1518)

A slightly different example, but making a similar point, is *Ezekiel's Vision* by Raphael. Here the vision itself, of God the Father borne up by the four "living creatures" and two angels, dominates the picture, magnificently and imposingly, but in the bottom left corner are two tiny human figures. One, presumably Ezekiel himself, is seen bathed in a stream of heavenly light, but the other seems unconscious either of the vision itself or of Ezekiel's inspiration. For the believer, the vision is, in our sense, mythical: a deep truth conveyed here in mythical form, but not something apparent to the eyes of history or science.

Myths should be seen as having their own validity and content. In what they tell us they reveal some aspect of what we need to know, religiously speaking. They are prisms, necessary prisms, through which some of the divine light might be refracted. The source of the light remains beyond what the myth can show us, and beyond what we can grasp. So, while valuing the myths for what they tell us, and our own myths in particular, we have to recognize the partiality of what each gives us, and the likelihood that other myths may also have much to teach us in their own ways. Thus, I am here and elsewhere reacting strongly against John Henry Newman's assertion in his *Apologia pro Vita Sua* that there are "but two alternatives, the road to Rome and the way to Atheism."[12] If that is

---

12. Newman, *Apologia pro Vita Sua* (1864), 204. I owe this reference to A. N. Wilson's *Confessions*, 224. My point against Newman and Catholic certainty is delightfully put by Rose Macaulay in *The Towers of Trebizon*, 182–83: "Nothing is as true as all that, and no faith can be delivered once and for all with without change.... [T]he truth, if it is ever discovered, means a long journey through a difficult jungle, with clearings every now and then, and paths that have to be hacked out as one walks, and dark lanterns swinging from the trees, and those lanterns are the light that has lighted every man, which can only come through the dark lanterns of our minds." And very appropriately to our theme, she goes on to speak of Ficino and the Florentine Academy lighting lamps before the bust of Plato, and being called heretics because they wanted the light of Greek learning let into church, and then Erasmus, Colet, and More also being called heretics for the same reason. But they, and their successors, knew that "if we stop trying to get fresh light into the Church, the Church will become dark and shut up." She adds, though, that human beings are "so strange and mixed"; according to her (and Foxe's *Book of Martyrs*), the same More who was for "humanism and fresh light in the Church" went on himself to burn people for heresy, even for erroneous opinions about the date of the final judgment. This latter claim, however, is now regarded as questionable. Though heretics were burned during More's chancellorship, his own involvement was probably, at most, indirect.

so, we are all doomed. I cherish the road to Rome, even while, like Dante, lost in a dark wood, and I have some respect for the way to atheism; but there are many possible routes between these two extremes, and many different terrains altogether. Many of these points in between and outside Newman's alternatives have aspects of truth about the transcendent, but none, not even Rome or atheism, could have the *only* truth.

Given that Islam is often thought of as being dogmatically literalist and exclusivist, it might seem surprising that there have been moments in its history when Muslim thinkers were espousing a view certainly more generous and possibly more intelligent than Newman's. Thus, in Andalusia in the thirteenth century Ibn al-'Arabi (1165–1240) taught that while the Absolute or God could not be defined or conceived, being literally no-thing, everything created, at its own level, was a manifestation of God. God or the Non-Delimited Being is manifested in myriad forms through which the light of being shines forth. Allah created the world as a mirror for his names and attributes, humanity being the polisher of that mirror. And this diversity of manifestation extends to a diversity of religious practices and perspectives, all of which have their own validity.

Both the universe itself and the prophets through the ages are the revelatory instruments of God: "We have sent no messenger. Save with the tongues of his people" (Qur'an 14.4). So, each people will have its own revelation and perspective. Ibn 'Arabi's attitude to religious diversity is summed up in his poem *Tarjuman al-ashwaq*:

> My heart has become capable of every form,
> it is a pasture for gazelles and a convent for Christian monks
> and a temple for idols and the pilgrim's Ka'ba
> and the tables of the Torah and the book of the Qur'an.
> I follow the religion of Love; whatever way Love's camels take,
> that is my religion and faith.

Ibn 'Arabi also uses the image of the bezels on a ring, each holding a precious stone. The bezels are all different, but they all stem from and point to the same interior, from which each of them draws

A Plenitude of Myths

their own shape and message. Different as each may seem, they are all connected to and draw existence from the same center.

Ibn 'Arabi had his Muslim critics, though he could not be condemned out of hand because his writings were suffused with quotations form the Qur'an and the Hadiths. But he also had his followers, of whom perhaps the most notable was the Yemeni Abd al-Karim al-Jili (1365–1424). Like Ibn 'Arabi, al-Jili emphasized both the unknowability of God in himself and the diversity of manifestations. Everything that exists worships God by its own nature. And this extends to the manifold of religious revelations throughout time and space: "The Real has a face in every object of worship . . . so only God is worshipped in every object of worship." Even the idol worshippers of Noah's time worshipped God, though they mistook the idol for the divinity itself. In all the different and diverse religions, "He [God] made appear within these religious communities the realities of His name and attributes. So He became manifest in all of them. . . ."

It has to be admitted that both Ibn 'Arabi and al-Jili would see Muhammad as the perfect man and the perfect prophet, whose revelation has a completeness lacking in others. Nevertheless, both found room for ultimate salvation for non-Muslims, and even for those who had repudiated Islam, which is surely consistent with their approach to religious diversity and the unknowability of the Godhead. Their eloquent reflections on these matters are very much to the point of this essay, and suggest that a recognition of the connection between the ultimate unknowability of God and religious diversity is neither of recent discovery nor confined to the West.[13]

To move to Thomistic mode for a moment, we can quote some of Thomas's own words that have a direct bearing on our theme:

> Sub diversis speciebus,
> Signum tantum and non rebus
> Latent res eximiae.

13. The passages from Ibn 'Arabi and al-Jili are quoted from Fitzroy Morrissey, "Abd al-Karim al-Jili's Sufi View of Other Religions," 176, 180, and 186.

("Under different forms wonderful things lie hidden, not the reality, but only the sign.") This is actually from a Eucharistic hymn written by Aquinas ("Lauda Sion Salvatorem"). The reality it refers to is Jesus's real presence, really there, rather than the sign. The sign is the appearance of bread and wine, which in the sacrament of the Mass has become the real presence of Christ. It might not be wholly against the spirit of Thomas's eucharistic thought to suggest that the different myths that mean so much religiously to so many people are themselves differing forms beneath which wonderful things lie hidden, the wonderful things being the reality beyond the forms or signs.

In 1899 the French philosopher and one-time priest Marcel Hébert heard this hymn during High Mass in the Duomo in Pisa, and was immediately struck: "Appearances, signs, symbols, which veil the mysterious reality, but which nevertheless adapt us to it, so that it penetrates us and makes us live—is not this one of the essential elements of all faith and all philosophy?"[14] Yes, I would reply, emphasizing the diversity of the appearances, signs and symbols that adapt their followers to the mysterious reality, making them live. The tragedy is that in 1907 this so-called "modernist" approach, which at the time was gaining adherents in the Catholic Church, was strongly condemned by Pope Pius X. This condemnation was then cruelly enforced, thus setting back any more generous approach within the Catholic Church to myth and reality for decades, if not for a century or more.

A rather more open-minded and, to my mind, more sensible approach to religious diversity has been expressed recently by Francis Clooney, a Jesuit theologian, who has immersed himself in Hindu thought and practice. Clooney refers to the early Jesuit missionaries to the Far East, who adopted the clothes and manners of the societies in which they worked, and to a limited degree some of their beliefs. But he advocates a far more open-minded attitude to non-Christian religion. Christians should approach non-Christian religions not just in the manner of making diplomatic concessions to non-Christians. They should do so in a genuinely open-minded

---

14. Hébert is quoted in Vidler, *A Variety of Catholic Modernists*, 49.

spirit, required by the Christian mission itself, as part of an honest attempt to detach the Christian message from the particular cultural contexts in which it has developed. Thus, the Christian must take these "foreign" religions to heart as part of the Christian mission itself, "believing that God *wants* this extreme learning to occur." Learning seriously outside the Christian context "remains well within the frame of Christian faith." It is so because one has a religious—in this case a Christian—duty "to learn religiously, in faith, beyond the boundaries of my faith." My faith is, of necessity, partial, even as it aspires to universal truth. So inherent in its very claim to truth is, or should be, an openness to other faiths, to other myths, just what Pius X in his crusade against "modernism" regrettably attempted to quash.[15]

I do not suppose that C. S. Lewis would have appreciated being called a theological modernist, but in a letter to Arthur Greeves on October 18, 1931, he spoke of the "pagan stories" as "God expressing Himself through the minds of the poets, using such images as He found there." He does add, rather like Ibn 'Arabi and al-Jili urging the completeness of Muhammad's prophecy, that Christianity is God expressing himself through "what we call 'real things,'" and so it is an (or the) ultimate revelation. But we could press Lewis here by suggesting that while the Christian myth may be based in historical events, its religious meaning is a matter of God expressing himself through images, images that are themselves an indirect expression of a transcendent truth beyond any adequate human expression, and thus *not a complete expression.*

Given the nature of divine transcendence, and the countervailing warnings from Kant and others about the problems involved in any would-be literal approach to that reality, and given also the plurality and diversity of religious myth in our world, we must be careful not to elevate any one myth—even "our" myth—to pre-eminence over all the others. So, while I praised the efforts of Ibn 'Arabi and al-Jili to make room for prophets other than Muhammad, I held back from their insistence that Muhammad's revelation was "complete." No revelation can be complete; all and

---

15. Clooney, "Beyond My God with God's Blessing," 90.

any may have elements of a truth that no one vision or version can capture.

This last thought has profound implications for religious conversion. It is perfectly understandable that someone brought up in one tradition might become so entranced by another that he or she commits him- or herself to that other tradition in a spirit of questing openness. We can also envisage people adopting a religion into which they were not born because they were attracted or convinced by certain aspects of its teaching which they had not found so clearly or evocatively articulated or practiced elsewhere. What, though, would be against the spirit of what is being argued here would be any form of dogmatic proselytizing, a forcible or aggressive assertion that one's own tradition has the whole or only truth, and that all the other myths were false, diabolical even. Thus, *extra ecclesiam, multae salutes*—outside the church there are many routes to salvation. Equally the attempt of Karl Rahner to solve the dilemma of the salvation of the virtuous unbaptized by referring to such people as "anonymous Christians" must be seen as condescending to them, and also unsound in the way it is taking Christianity to be ultimately the only route to salvation or indeed to religious truth more generally.

Very much what I am trying to argue here was well expressed a century and a half ago by the American theologian Horace Bushnell. In his book *God in Christ* he wrote:

> When God is revealed, He will not, if He is truly and efficiently revealed, be cleared of obscurity and mystery. He will not be a bald, philosophic unity, perfectly comprehended and measured by us. . . . [I]f we have no questions about Him . . . [He is] revealed away, not revealed. No; if He is revealed at all, it will be through infinite repugnances and contrarieties; through forms, colors, motions, words, persons, or personalities; all presenting themselves to our sense and feeling, to pour in something of the divine into our nature. And a vast circle of mystery will play and glitter in living threads of motion, as lightning on a cloud; and what they themselves do not reveal of God, the mystery will—a Being infinite,

undiscovered, undiscoverable, therefore true. But if we could see the last boundaries of God, and hold Him clear of a question within the molds of logic and cognition, then He is not God any longer, we have lost the conception of God.[16]

While a Wittgensteinian fact might be truly and efficiently revealed, clear of obscurity and mystery, the very distance between God and human conceptions of things implies that a "true and efficient" approach to God will always be replete with difficulty, complexity, and even doubt, certainly doubts to its adequacy. Truths about God are, to refer to Pascal again, truths of the heart, not of geometry, but they are not necessarily less true because of that. Even within the *Lebenswelt*, there are realities sought and understood by the heart, whose logic and cognition is not that of natural science. Even more is this the case when we are approaching the divine, illuminated by rays of divine revelation.

It might be objected at this point that there could not be differing accounts of the same ultimate reality, all worthy of being entertained or even believed. After all, belief by its nature aims at truth, and this basic truism has implications for the extent to which competing accounts of the truth to which a particular belief is aiming can be envisaged or regarded as acceptable. The cat can't both be on the mat and not on the mat, so if I believe the one proposition, I must reject the other. This is, of course, the picture of language and indeed of belief that is impressed on us by the *Tractatus* account of the early Wittgenstein and by many philosophers in thrall to scientific accounts of reality. Actually, I would introduce some qualifying thoughts even here. We are by now, a century after the stirrings of quantum theory, long accustomed to the thought that our human forms of description and theorizing are unable unequivocally to capture basic realities in the quantum world. Niels Bohr himself speculated that quantum reality was beyond our powers of comprehension, and that, in Popper's words, "understandable reality ended where classical physics ended."[17]

16. Bushnell, *God in Christ*, 144–45.
17. On Bohr, see Popper, *Quantum Theory and the Schism in Physics*, 9–10.

The Prism of Truth

In fact, we do not have to delve into the mysteries of quantum physics to understand that even the most straightforward description of the table before me will inevitably be partial, in focusing on some aspects of that object and excluding others. To say "everything" about that table would be an endless and incompletable task, as there are countless ways of describing and looking at it, and innumerably many ways of analyzing what it is, its structure, its composition, and so on. In focusing on some aspects rather than on others we will be producing an account or description that for the purposes for which it is intended simplifies the whole or even overlooks aspects of it. Back in the early seventeenth century Galileo himself told us that in the new science he was pioneering we should look at phenomena simply in terms of their size, shape, position, and quantity of motion. Qualities such as color, sound, smell, taste, and feel would not be part of the descriptions and explanations offered by the new physics, and with few exceptions scientists ever since have followed him. Does this mean these phenomenal qualities of the table before me are unimportant or do not really exist? I would prefer to say that both the scientific and the everyday "phenomenal" or experiential account are true as far as they go, but neither is the whole truth, and neither should be treated as inherently superior to the other. Each has its place and its purpose, and each can have part of the truth, depending on what we are trying to do.

However, whatever we say about partial truth in describing the world of everyday experience, things become *far more fuzzy* when approaching transcendent reality, where it is generally agreed that no human account of something so far beyond our comprehension can be complete. In the words of Pico della Mirandola, the Florentine Neoplatonist, "divine things must be concealed under enigmatic veils and poetic dissimulation."[18] Even though the clouds can be seen through up to a point, there is always the danger that we humans may be blinded by too direct a shaft of

---

18. Pico della Mirandola, quoted from Eugenio Garin, *Pico della Mirandola* (Rome: Edizioni di Storia e Letteratura, 2011), 581, in Wind, *Pagan Mysteries in the Renaissance*, 123.

A Plenitude of Myths

divine sunlight (as happened to Goethe's reawakened Faust, who had to look into a colored reflection of the sun). So the veils are not just because of our intellectual or spiritual limitations. They also have a protective, loving aspect. Once it is seen, for both positive and negative reasons, that our access to the divine is necessarily veiled, even clouded, it becomes clear that any account—my or your account or picture—is *necessarily partial*.

What truth there is in any account (or myth) is far from being the whole truth, which opens the door to envisaging the value in and even the truth in other accounts or myths with other aspects of the whole truth or different emphases on the truths that are shared. Where these mythical accounts appear to be in conflict, the conflicts may be resolved at a deeper level. For example, the notion of the incarnation in Christianity can be seen in terms of God taking on the experience of human suffering and death, something with its own resonance in Hinduism. Do Judaism and Islam deny such an intimate divine involvement in our fallen world? Does Christianity pay sufficient account to the absolute otherness of God, which we find articulated in Islam? Maybe some reconciliation of these apparent differences can be effected, or at least a route toward such a reconciliation. (And so with other differences between the various world faiths, as the Jesuit Fr. Clooney implies in his talk of learning "outside" the Christian faith.) Maybe the explicit statements of the myths, while pointing to realities, are not literally true (as we have seen Aquinas, among others argue). Maybe we cannot, as Lewis admitted, say "in cold prose" just what the myths mean. But they are strikingly evocative, suggestive of a or the reality we glimpse only partially. We could well urge that if the explicit statements of the myths were not suggestive of something real, they would lack the power they evidently have. I am not giving answers to these questions; indeed, I cannot. Here I am simply suggesting the sorts of explorations and conversations that might arise when apparently conflicting myths are brought into comparison with each other. The conflicts could then be seen as contraries (of emphasis, of suggestion), rather than as contradictories in the formal logical sense.

Further, as human expressions, these myths and traditions may well have become entangled with misconceptions and even falsehoods, as, following Peter Hacker, we have suggested earlier. Thoughtful and sympathetic reflection might lead believers to understand elements of their own tradition as such, and move back from them. In the present context, one such falsehood would be to insist that my myth contains the whole or complete truth, to the exclusion of all the others. What I am arguing here is for a mid-course between cognitive agnosticism regarding myth (what we seem to find in Hick) and a dogmatic assertion of the primacy of one myth over all the others. The latter position should be ruled out by the nature of divine transcendence, while the former overlooks the way that myths and the visions they give us can point us beyond pure agnosticism. They can indeed intimate to our human minds aspects of the divine reality beyond and beneath our everyday world.

In doing this, the myths with which I am concerned in this essay are characteristically embedded in traditions not just of thought but also of worship and practice. So they not only give us insight into the nature of the divine, they also show us how to approach this reality in prayer and contemplation, and also in how in the presence of this reality we should lead our lives ethically and morally. For these practical reasons believers will tend to engage in the practices and communities of the myths to which they have been accustomed or to which they have been drawn. In so acting they will give form and content to what they have been moved to accept, through their upbringing or later religious experience or practice. Their myth will rightly be seen as that which has framed and structured their religious life and the terms in which they see the divine. They will naturally feel at home within it. But, I am arguing, they should engage with their religious community and its myth with a sense that theirs is not in an absolute sense the only or the final route to the divine.

In a letter to Kathleen Raine, Lewis wrote that "what flows into you from [the] myth is not truth but reality (truth is always about something but reality is about which truth is) and therefore

A Plenitude of Myths

every myth becomes the father of innumerable truths on the abstract level."[19] The point surely is that these truths, even if ultimately expressible in abstract mode, can be approached only via the minds of the prophets and poets. In myth an abstract truth becomes imaginable, and thus meaningful and motivating. If all that we drew from a myth was an abstract truth or truths, then the myth itself reduces to mere allegory, without its essential open-endedness, to which its enigmatic, mysterious, and at time baffling quality is an indication. And, following on from this, we could ask whence came the images to the minds of the poets and prophets.

Seemingly providing an answer to this last question, Tolkien, Lewis's colleague, friend, and sparring partner, spoke of humanity as not wholly lost. Under God, humanity is a sub-creator, "the refracted light through whom is splintered from a single White to many hues, and endlessly combined in living shapes that move from mind to mind." Our myths are limited, or even misguided in parts, but they "steer, however shakily, to the true harbour." They are, in Tolkien's view, not travelers' tales, beast stories, or dream adventures, but revelatory of this world and leading to consolation in the form of "a joy beyond the walls of this world, poignant with grief, a sudden glimpse of the underlying reality or truth."[20] One could insist that these myths and their consolations are all wish fulfillment, disparaging them as illusory and sentimental fictions cowardly people invent against the dark and doubt. But this line of thought leaves unexplained how here on earth our hearts are endlessly restless, and notions of a perfect other world are well-nigh universal in human culture and history. It also leaves unexplained where the notions come from or came from in the first place.

As is well-known, Descartes in his Third Meditation takes very seriously the question of how human beings, encircled in the enclosure of their own "I think," could come to regard themselves

---

19. Quoted by Wilson, *C. S. Lewis: A Biography*, 219.

20. See Tolkien, "On Fairy Stories." The passage about refracted light comes from the poem in the section on Fantasy, and its reference to breathing a lie through silver refers to C. S. Lewis's comment on Tolkien view of myth in the Addison's walk conversation. The "sudden glimpse" passage is in the epilogue. The "splintered fragment" is quoted by H. Carpenter in *J. R. R. Tolkien*, 151.

as limited and imperfect. An idea of imperfection is necessarily contrasted with an idea of perfection, the finite with the infinite. But how could we, as limited beings, ever come up with the idea of perfection, of a perfect Being, an infinity, against which we measure ourselves and compare our imperfection with its perfection? The cause of an idea we have must be at least as real as the idea itself. And so, within our own limited existence, it is the perfect Being who causes us to think of his existence in contrast to our own imperfection.

This is not the place to attempt a full defense of Descartes's argument. But while it is widely dismissed by philosophical critics, his argument does raise a significant question about our human sense that there are, even if not in this world, perfect realities and a genuine infinity. Indeed, the very questions that Descartes raises in his systematically doubting the truth of what he believes (the program of the so-called Cartesian doubt) would presuppose that there is something real, something true, against which he is comparing the beliefs he has. This something real, this standard against which he is measuring his beliefs, must be perfect and changeless and true in a way his own shifting thoughts are not. Yet he has this notion as the veiled accompaniment to his skepticism. Where does he (or where do we) get these ideas of perfection and truth from? This is the question that has its roots in Pythagorean thought and that Plato wrestles with throughout his philosophy; and Descartes's point is in its way Platonic. Furthermore, following John Cottingham, we can also point out that at the end of the Third Meditation Descartes asks the reader (or fellow meditator) to allow him to "pause for while, and gaze at, and wonder at, and adore the beauty of this immense light, in so far as my darkened intellect can bear it." The immense light is that which gives us an intimation of perfection, pulling us toward it and forcing us to compare our own thoughts with it. It is the burden of this essay that it is not so much by reason as through myth that our darkened intellect begins to gaze, wonder, and adore.[21]

---

21. Cottingham, *Philosophy of Religion*, 12.

A PLENITUDE OF MYTHS

What I would suggest here is that Descartes's question about the cause and origin of the philosophical idea of perfection can equally well be raised in connection with our myths of perfection, telling of joys beyond the walls of this world. Are these simply byproducts of the mentality of creatures randomly evolved in a dead, valueless, and ultimately meaningless cosmos? Or are they, through us, part of the web of stories the universe tells itself? Stories suggesting that the physical universe is not the whole of reality? A web spun by many voices, in many ways, but a *revelatory* web, inspired by or through a reality beyond itself?

7

A Florentine Story
Christian Platonism in the Renaissance

WE MAY THINK OF this positive recognition of religious diversity as a particularly contemporary insight. It is true that the opening up of the world intellectually and imaginatively has sharpened the need for a recognition of the fact of religious and mythological diversity, and of the benefits to understanding that such diversity allows. But, as we have just seen, we are not the first generation to think in this way. Indeed, the very idea of a hidden God, a God whose ways are in many ways inscrutable and less than self-evident, which is surely implicit in much of Christianity (and in other traditions too, in medieval and Kabbalistic Judaism, for example), also lends itself easily to the possibility of manifold revelations and multiple mythological approaches to the divine.[1] So too would the

---

1. It might be worth underlining here that the religiously fruitful notion of a "hidden" God, a God whose workings are far from obvious on the surface of things, and at times apparently problematic, need not imply that, as with the Tao discussed earlier (see fn 12 above), there is not some drive within us, a reasonable drive to boot, to conceive the world and our existence as divinely created. That this drive, and responses to it, seem to be firmly embedded in most of human history and culture may reduce the force of the atheistical line of argument that it is puzzling that a loving creator has not given to us humans signs of his existence. Signs of one sort or another do seem to be perceived by

classic Neoplatonic notion (derived from *Parmenides*, esp. 141e ff.) of the One beyond Being, above all things, but from which all that exists comes, is sustained, and tends toward. In other words, this One brings about a plurality of manifestations in the realm of Being, and also a plurality of myths and theological conceptions.

Ideas about the intellectual and spiritual benefits of religious diversity have been present in Western Christianity before now. This was no more so than in late fifteenth-century Florence, where Lorenzo de' Medici himself averred that "without Plato it would be hard to be a good Christian or a good citizen." Timothy Verdon, from whom I quote this phrase, emphasizes that Lorenzo is not here invoking a humanist and non- or anti-Christian counterculture (as Jacob Burckhardt thought), so much as saying that Plato can enhance and enlighten the Christianity that was all pervasive at the time. Among modern thinkers, Simone Weil more than any other has explored the connections between Christian and ancient Greek thought. In doing this, she suggested that during the time of the Florentine Renaissance "the Greeks of classical times, Pythagoras, Plato, then became the objects of a religious veneration

---

the majority of humanity, often, of course, through myth, which is in some way the burden of this essay. Of course, asserting this does not mean that these signs should be those invoked by Cleanthes in part 3 of David Hume's *Dialogues Concerning Natural Religion*, namely, of a great voice from the sky speaking good sense in different languages. Such a suggestion—which seems to be what some atheists want—trivializes the meaning of a religious attitude to the world, reducing it to a very worldly conception of God and making our worship of that divinity no different from succumbing to some human ruler in a position of power over us. In contrast, we should recall the words of the LORD in Exodus 33:20: "Thou canst not see my face and live, for there shall be no man see me and live." In other words, our very survival depends on the fullness of the divine light being occluded from us, even at times being replaced by a dark night of emptiness and doubt—a dark night that can descend over us without actually or objectively diminishing the signs of divinity in the universe. On the point about multiple incarnations of the hidden God, it is interesting to note that Aquinas himself does not rule out the possibility, rejecting it only on grounds of revelation (see *Summa Theologiae* 3.3.7). Admitting multiple incarnations, or at least their possibility, would also help to bring Eastern and Western mythologies closer together. It would also emphasize the way incarnation of the divine is, from a Christian point of view, written into the fabric of the universe, so to speak.

that went in perfect harmony with the Christian faith," though she adds, perhaps tendentiously, that this attitude of mind was only of brief duration.²

We can take as representative of the best of the thought of that time and place the Christian Neoplatonist Marsilio Ficino. He was highly influential, not just in Florence, but throughout fifteenth- and sixteenth-century Europe, including in the England of John Colet and Thomas More. Germane to our general argument here is the way in which Ficino places joy above vision and argues that the soul acquires more divine goodness by love than it does by knowledge.³ Ficino is not saying that knowledge is not important, but rather that the knowledge that is most important is the highest form of knowledge predicated by Plato, namely, that infused with beauty and goodness. In an amalgam of the Platonic One and the Christian beatific vision, Ficino presents it as a knowledge that moves our deepest desires and attracts the highest level of our being, a knowledge of the heart, a finessed knowledge. Further, it is a type of knowledge that unifies apparently disparate themes, as does the best type of myth, and brings them into touch with our inner feelings and reactions, often over spans of centuries. As Verdon points out, it is also the type of knowledge sought in the

---

2. Verdon, "Christianity, the Renaissance and the Study of History," 2. Simone Weil's statement is from *The Need for Roots*, 285.

3. See Wind, *Pagan Mysteries of the Renaissance*, 79. My interpretation of Ficino and of Gemistus Plethon is indebted to Wind, and also to Robichaud, *Plato's Persona: Marsilio Ficino, Renaissance Humanism and Platonic Tradition*. The quotations and references to both Ficino and Plethon are taken from Wind and Robichaud, where full bibliographical details can be found. While we are focusing here on Ficino and fifteenth-century Florence, it is worth underlining that the Renaissance interest in ancient pagan thought, and the attempted recovery then of what was thought of as the wisdom of ancient Egypt, Persia, and Greece, and the teaching of such in universities, no doubt had its influence on the missionaries of the sixteenth and seventeenth centuries who studied, often sympathetically and with a degree of deferential respect, the religion and thought of the native peoples of Latin America, Japan, China, and South Asia. At times this interest led to attempts to marry Christian thought to the religions of the peoples the missionaries worked among, even if this was not warmly received by the official churches. On this point, see Hankins, "The Significance of Renaissance Philosophy," 341–42.

A FLORENTINE STORY

internal spirituality preached by the mendicant orders from the twelfth century on, a knowledge that would put us in touch with the scenes in the Gospels and other sacred texts. This knowledge would have its artistic counterpart in the art that increasingly relied on perspective and expressive gestures to make the believing perceiver feel part of the scene he was contemplating.

Ficino was for the most part an orthodox Christian—indeed, he was and remained an ordained priest. But he was influenced by the Neoplatonism that had reentered Europe when Gemistus Plethon, the legendary Byzantine scholar from Mistra, attended the Council of Ferrara in 1438. In Ficino's view, the Christian religion does not possess the sole and exclusive way to mediate between humanity and the divine. In this, he was following Plethon, who, perhaps more Platonic than Christian, had argued that if the truths of Christianity were fundamental, they would not have been withheld before Christ's time.[4] In a telling image Plotinus, from the third century AD, had earlier compared the Soul's reasons (*logoi*) in the universe to a living net immersed in the waters of an immeasurably vast sea that spreads its reach into ever-expanding waters. Augustine had spoken of what we now call the Christian religion—*res ipsa* (the thing itself), as he put it—as being "with the ancients, and with the human race from its beginning to the time when Christ appeared in the flesh: from when on the true religion, *which already existed* [my italics], began to be called the Christian."[5] And, as we have already noted, Aquinas himself contemplated the possibility of more than one incarnation (rejecting it only on grounds of revelation), which is itself indicative of a sense

---

4. See Robichaud, *Plato's Persona*, 241. The Plotinus reference that follows is discussed by Robichaud in the same place. On Plethon's influence in the Italian Renaissance, it is noteworthy that Ficino refers to Plethon as "the second Plato" in his translation of Plotinus's *Enneads*, while Cosimo de Medici founded the Academy at Florence in Plethon's honor. In 1465 Sigismondo Malatesta took Plethon's body from his tomb in Mistra and reburied it in a splendid sarcophagus in the peristyle of the Malatesta Temple in Rimini, where it can still be seen. (See Runciman, *Mistra*, 116–17.) On Plethon's views about the timelessness of the Christian myth, see Wind, *Pagan Mysteries of the Renaissance*, 245.

5. Augustine, *Retractiones*, I, xiii.

The Prism of Truth

in which incarnation or *the* incarnation is an eternal reality. He glossed this thought about incarnation with the observation that the divine person is infinite, and cannot be limited by any existing thing, which I would venture to suggest could include being limited to any one existing myth.[6]

In line with this ecumenical approach to the divine, Ficino—a Christian priest, remember—would argue that there was no great gap between Christian revelation and myth and what would be referred to as the pagan myths of which he was aware. He thus found that the Neoplatonists—such as Plotinus, Amelius, Porphyry, Iamblichus, Theodore, and Proclus—believed like him in the soul being created with a nature like that of God and able to return to God in contemplation. He saw a continuity between his own brand of Neoplatonic Christianity and the mythical thinking of Zoroaster, Hermes, Orpheus, Aglaophamus, Pythagoras, and, of course, Plato himself, particularly in regard to the immortality of the soul. All were part of a *prisca theologica*, an ancient theological strain, which would also embrace ancient Egyptian mysteries, as expressed in the *Chaldean Oracles*. All these in one way or another moved from creation or emanation, through a worldly fall, to redemption and resurrection and a return to the One.

A striking visual encapsulation of the same intuition is to be found in no less a place than the ceiling of the Sistine Chapel itself. No doubt, as art historians will tell us, the whole project was intended to glorify the papacy, idealize the human body, and also to represent earlier phases of salvation history as finding their fulfillment in Christ. It may well have been all these things, but the way Michelangelo depicts these earlier phases and figures lets us wonder whether they do not have their own validity as they are in themselves, and not only as precursors of Christianity. The earlier phases are not just the Old Testament scenes of the creation and the flood, but also involve the pagan ignudi, naked wingless angels who seem to be supporting and holding the whole drama together.

---

6. Aquinas, *Summa Theologiae*, 3.3.7.

Some ignudi from Michelangelo's Sistine Chapel ceiling

Pagan they may have been in inspiration, but the human body is still in a sense divine, as created by God in his likeness (Genesis 1:17), and then taken on by Christ (as Dante emphasizes). Even more significant, representatives of earlier time are the oracles or sybils from Persia, Erythraea, Delphi, Cumae, and Libya. To my mind at least, these ancient sources of revelation are depicted as figures of wisdom and hope in their own right, infused with grace, and exuding insight.

The Sistine ignudi will perhaps recall the naked figures in Michelangelo's earlier painting, the so-called Doni Tondo. These figures disport themselves behind a wall in front of which we see the Holy Family; behind, yes, but also with their own value and beauty, which should remind us that Michelangelo himself moved in Florentine Neoplatonic circles. For Michelangelo, while we have to escape from our imperfect bodily existence, in a perfected or risen state the human body is the best picture of the human soul (which he shows in his representations of the risen Christ and indeed in the elect in his *Last Judgement*); and we can get an inkling of this in the bodily beauty we sometimes see even in our fallen existence, in some real people and in the ideal forms of ancient sculpture, with which Michelangelo was obsessed.

The Prism of Truth

The Delphic oracle from Michelangelo's Sistine Chapel ceiling

Michelangelo, *Doni Tondo* (1504-6)

One could certainly speculate that if Ficino and the Christian Neoplatonists of his time had knowledge of Hindu and Buddhist myths and practices, they would have been able to accommodate them as well in a *philosophia perennis*, though one free from the gnostic and hermetic elements that often attached to this idea at the turn of the twentieth century, myth without Golden Dawn mystification, so to speak.

The myths of which Ficino wrote all point to a One, an eternal, divine source. In contrast to the stoicism we encountered in the ancient atomists, they show this God as involved with and in humanity, even to the extent of taking on human form in an incarnation of one sort or another. A morality of individuality and community develops naturally from such images and ideas, with "gods in human form saving and helping men," as Ficino put it in his commentary on Paul's Epistle to the Romans, where he also cites Plato's *Laws* (716c) as saying against Protagoras (and, in effect, against modern Enlightenment thinkers) that *God*, not man, is the measure of all things, especially if God becomes man.[7]

This gloss about God becoming man may be Platonically uncanonical, but it was one sanctioned by a number of Neoplatonic commentators, such as Amelius and the Pseudo-Dionysius, as well as Ficino himself, apart, of course, from its appearance at the beginning of the Gospel of John, a text that bears marks of Hellenistic influence: "And the Word (*Logos*) was made flesh, and dwelt amongst us, and we beheld his glory, the glory as of the only begotten of the Father" (John 1:14). Interestingly, Ficino himself believed that the Pythagoreans rejected the Platonic doctrine of the divided line, whereby material things below the line were cut off from the perfect and immaterial divine above it; for Ficino and the Pythagoreans each section of the divided line has a divine source.[8]

The Pythagorean procession of being thus anticipates the Christian idea of incarnation. It is also clear that any divine

---

[7]. See Robichaud, *Plato's Persona*, 196–200, esp. 199–200, where the passage from the Romans commentary is quoted. The Romans passage is to be found in Ficino's *Opera Omnia* (1576), vol. 1, 431. On the idea that our notions of right and wrong are not invented by us, but come to us from the depths of reality itself, contrast J. L. Mackie's influential (and Darwinian) treatise *Ethics: Inventing Right and Wrong*, whose title tells us all we need to know about what has become a very popular attitude to morality, but one that hardly does justice to what we know, deep down, when confronted with absolute evil or absolute good. These things force their nature on us, in ways that cannot be explained in term of our own constructions or inventions.

[8]. See Robichaud, *Plato's Persona*, 185. In *Pythagoras and the Doctrine of Transmigration*, James Luchte argues strongly for a clear difference between Plato and the Pythagoreans on this point. For the most part, Plato sees life on earth as primarily an attempt to escape the material and the realm of becoming and return to the timeless immaterial One. In contrast to Plato's predominant downgrading of the material, in Luchte's view the Pythagoreans see positive value in our earthly existence, and the material an essential aspect of the All, to which in becoming it can be attuned. If this is right, one could argue further that the Christian concept of divine incarnation has more in common with Pythagoreanism than with Platonism.

embrace of human form must encompass the whole of humanity, and so must militate against any tyrannical or caste system, which would oppress or exclude segments of humanity from proper treatment. It will also militate against the way the Athenian ambassadors are depicted in Thucydides's so-called Melian dialogue. In attempting to cower the Melians into submission during the Peloponnesian War, and prior to destroying them, the Athenians tell their opponents that it is a universal law of nature according to which the strong must thrive and the weak suffer what they must. It is clear that Thucydides is hostile to the way the Athenians are acting and speaking—as proto-Darwinians, so to speak—even if it is true that a counter-Darwinian insight became fully explicit only with the advent of Christianity. (As Simone Weil forcefully demonstrates, it is not true that a critique of the "universal law of nature" begins only with Christianity: a careful reading of Homer, Aeschylus, and Euripides, to say nothing of Thucydides's forensically objective treatment of the Melian dialogue, suggests that the ancient Greeks, the Athenian spokesmen notwithstanding, had already moved away from any crude social Darwinism long before the birth of Christ.)

Ficino's conception is of a noetic light touching and awakening our intellect. The divine enlightenment that thus moves us is non-discursive, of a different and higher order than that of our ordinary reasoning, and it may be explicitly symbolic. As he puts it, "the divine is not discovered by us but rather is revealed from above."[9] Ficino himself distrusts written accounts of this noetic inspiration. Even its oral transmission is to be treated with caution, and he generally enjoins a sacred silence in these matters. I would not dissent from the notion that beyond any exposition or symbols we will be left with an awed silence, but I would fill out what Ficino says by suggesting that sacred myths will play a key role in the reception of noetic light. They are the media by which its deliverances reach us. It is through our imaginative reception of these myths that we begin to become aware of the nature, structure, and

---

9. From Ficino's argumentum on Plato's *Seventh Letter*, as quoted by Robichaud, *Plato's Persona*, 222. (*Opera Omnia*, vol. 2, 1532)

reality of the divine, and its connection with and embedding in the superficially disconnected elements of our experience. It is this dawning of noetic light that C. S. Lewis responded to instinctively on hearing of Balder, Adonis, and Bacchus, and which he did not immediately comprehend in hearing of Christ.

Ficino does not confine his talk of myth to those that emerge unauthored from the depths of time. Plato himself is an inspired mythmaker (mythopoetis). Of the myth of the *Timaeus* Ficino writes in his commentary on that dialogue: "For he fabricates this myth appropriately in imitation of Pythagorean myths," going on to say that he writes "so that we do not accept these things as though they were historical truth."[10] There are, of course, many myths in Plato's writings, most of which touch on our relationship to the divine, of our descent from the divine and out ascent back to it, and we do accept them, or can accept them, even though they are not presented as historical truth. Why does Plato speak

---

10. See Robichaud, *Plato's Persona*, 157 (*Opera Omnia*, vol. 2, 1466). Pythagorean and other Greek myths may not be historical truth, and we can appreciate their weight and significance while discounting any sense that they might also be historically true, as C. S. Lewis did with Balder and the rest. But what about the Christian myth? Suppose that it were established that it was all a fabrication from the second century AD, without any true historical roots, could we still see it as *mythologically* true? I think not, for two reasons. The first is that the New Testament presents itself as a historical document, about things seen and experienced by real people in a definite time and place. So, discovering that it was actually a fabrication would severely damage its credibility. Then, secondly, and more fundamentally, on the view I am articulating, a divine immersion in the human world is key. It had to happen, really and not mythologically, at least once. Now, I have argued that the *significance* of the incarnation is eternal—in the telling phrase of Thomas Bradwardine, "God's grace is already (always) present in time as in nature, before any good works existed." But, while the significance and reach of the incarnation (the ultimate good work) is eternal, its *efficacy and meaning* depends on its actually happening historically at least once. The claim of Christianity is that divine incarnation happened in first-century Judaea. So, although the events described in the Gospels have a truly kairotic significance, that significance depends on their real-time historicity, which is what is taught in the New Testament and in the Christian tradition. So, if we are to regard Christianity and the New Testament as mythically true, we *also* have to see what they describes as really happening in historical time, as described in the New Testament. (I thank Tim Mawson for stimulating my thinking on this point.)

in myth, rather than in down-to-earth descriptions and ordinary language analyses, as Aristotle might have done? I conjecture that it was both because Plato wanted to engage our imagination and because what he writes about cannot be discursively described or grasped.

The myths he uses draw on earlier religious themes and moods, and so have a quasi-religious resonance. They do not present us with a logically water-tight account of the divine; no such thing is possible, and using different myths allows him to emphasize different aspects of what would seem a series of contradictions if laid out in discursive form. In this area, while contradictories are not to be countenanced, contraries can sometimes each have part of the truth, as we suggested earlier in arguing that the divinity itself must encompass and sublimate poles that, on the surface at least, are in tension (such as mercy and justice, immanence and transcendence, even spirit and matter). Mahler, a composer who strove to reconcile manifold tensions and contrasting moods in his work, used to counsel against too hasty an assertion by saying, "Sometimes the opposite is also true." In developing his different mythological accounts of the divine and in exploiting their half-remembered religious sources, Plato gives no sense that one supersedes or replaces another, whatever tension there might be between the different accounts if laid side by side. Each makes sense in its own terms, and we do not feel in thinking about the totality of the myths that we are entwined in contradictions, so much as standing like Wittgenstein on the shore of a powerful and illimitable ocean, only part of which we can survey at any one time, and which our descriptions necessarily over-simplify and reduce.

Ficino sees Plato's mythologizing not only as having Pythagorean roots. He also associated it with Asia (through the Zoroaster who wrote the Chaldean Oracles, according to Plethon), with Africa (through Hermes), and with Europe (through Orpheus). So in his thought Plato encompassed all the known world of his time, and not just the thought of his own locality and tradition—or perhaps better, he saw his tradition as having universal roots. Socrates, Plato's teacher, may have been apophatic, but he was not atheistical. He too was a mythmaker, seeing the body as a tomb, but through the soul joined to God. The soul of a weak and or a bad man is like a leaky jar, unable to retain anything, and suffering from an insatiable appetite (see *Gorgias* 492–93). As he is about to die, Socrates refers to Apollo's swans, who, endowed with prophetic insight, sing "because they know the good things that await them in the unseen world. . . . I am in the same service as the swans, and dedicated to the same god" (*Phaedo* 85b). Ficino extemporizes on this passage, seeing Socrates singing and playing the lyre as he awaits death, attuning his soul to the divine harmony, in the manner of Pythagoras, Empedocles, and Orpheus.[11]

Socrates and Plato are, of course, historical figures, whose mythmaking (*mythopoeia*) is a matter of record. It is, though, telling that Plato gives precedence to the ancients: "The men of old . . . were better than ourselves, and dwelt nearer the gods," particularly in the way they thought about the relationship between the one and the many. "Your clever modern man" though, races straight from the one to the unlimited many, thus allowing the intermediaries to escape him, "whereas it is the recognition of those intermediaries that makes all the difference between a philosophical and a contentious discussion" (*Philebus* 16c–17a).

Allan Bloom sums up the ancient Greek approach to philosophical speculation about such matters as the one and the many or change and permanence thus: "The Greeks, notoriously unmethodical, . . . possessed a rich natural consciousness of nature in its immediate concreteness. That is the proper beginning point. The theories and concepts can thus be tested against such a consciousness; a very large part of that concrete consciousness is encapsulated in their abundance and richness of myth."[12] Shades perhaps

---

11. Robichaud, *Plato's Persona*, 161 (*Opera Omnia*, vol. 1, 652).

12. Bloom, "The Crisis of Liberal Education," 358. It is worth noting here that Bloom is insistent that a true liberal education will look at the Greek approaches to mathematics, the natural world, philosophy, politics, history, tragedy, and the rest as they are in themselves; but in themselves the ancient Greek approaches to all these subjects—including science, as we saw in our discussion of ancient atomism—address the most fundamental questions facing us as human beings. They all address moral questions, in other words, questions that are also probed with haunting resonance in their mythology.

of Tolkien's view that myths are a trace of the understanding we had before the fall, and also of Wittgenstein's attacks on the modern empirico-rationalist "craving for generality," which precisely glosses over the complexities and nuances of the subject matter. Over and above this, Plato is giving us a salutary warning about always thinking that we moderns are more rational and more enlightened than those we may dismiss as mere mythologizers from an endarkened prehistory.

But does this mean that old myths are always to be preferred to new ones? Can new myths be made, with the imaginative qualities of the old ones? Matthew Arnold lamented about the loss to modern writers of the terrible old mythic story already in the spectator's mind before he or she entered the theatre, standing as a group of statuary, faintly seen, at the end of a long vista. In like vein, commenting on the poetry of T. S. Eliot, George Seferis wrote that "when myth was a common feeling the poet had at his disposal a living medium, a ready emotional atmosphere where he could move freely and approach his fellow men."[13] Obviously Plato, even in his philosophical persona, was making use of the ready emotional atmosphere of which Seferis speaks. We could add that it is not just the poet who has this ability, but anyone who is in thrall to a religious myth, which is why the loss of myth in a culture is so enfeebling, humanly and spiritually.

This loss Wagner, W. B. Yeats, Tolkien, and Lewis himself, among many others, have tried to remedy, which raises the question as to whether it is still possible to create a new myth with the same power as the ancient and life-forming myths we have been considering in this essay. In thinking that it might be possible, we could point out similarities and analogies between well-traveled myths and those created by writers and artists of recent times. Thus, to take a striking example of a modern myth, perhaps the most striking of all, we could look at Wagner's *Ring of the Nibelung*, which is not only set in a mythical landscape, but draws quite explicitly on ancient Icelandic and Germanic mythology. Not only

---

13. Seferis, *A Poet's Journal*, 45.

that, but there are in Wagner's recasting of these myths, themes very close to Christian and ancient Greek myths.

There is, for example, an original sin, when the malignant dwarf Alberich renounces love and violently seizes worldly power, which destroys the natural innocence of the world. There is a divine character (Brünnhilde, daughter of Wotan, the ruling god), who out of compassionate love for Sieglinde, a suffering human being, renounces her divinity to become fully human, and ultimately a willing victim. There is the God (Wotan) who withdraws from the world and sends his own offspring to redeem it. There is the very Christian message that redemption, personal and collective, can come about only through love and the renunciation of power and gold. And in the character of Brünnhilde there is the very Greek sense that the intervention of divinity into the temporal world is likely to be transformative and subversive. (In Greek mythology we have Medea and Phaedra, both semi-divinities, whose desperate furor wreaks tragedy and havoc on those around them.)

No doubt, consciously or unconsciously, Wagner drew on all these and many other well-established mythical themes and patterns. It is also true, as he said himself, that he hoped through art (*his* art) to "salvage the kernel of religion, inasmuch as the mythical images which religion would wish to be believed as true are apprehended in art for their symbolic value, and through ideal representations of those symbols art reveals the concealed deep truth within them."[14] The revelation of "concealed deep truths" within religious myths would be consistent with the general line of myth that I am here proposing.

Against this, in Wagner's case at least, it could be urged that Wagner's own position actually denies that there is a God or gods. His works are intended rather to show how the moral and political implications of religious myth can be brought out as purely human realities. We can thus see the need for compassion, love, and renunciation of worldly power and ambition in a purely human context, and even interpret redemption as wrought by ourselves. "Redemption to the Redeemer" are the closing words of Wagner's

---

14. Wagner, "Die Religion und die Kunst," 211.

A Florentine Story

Parsifal (*Erlösung der Erlöser*), the most obvious interpretation of which is that the redeemer is Parsifal, the purely human knight, who redeems by his learning through pain and experience of the necessity in our lives of compassion and forgiveness; though quite who or what he redeems remains something of an enigma. Parsifal is Christ-like in key ways, but he is not Christ, and he is certainly not the second "person" of the Blessed Trinity. On this widely held interpretation, Wagner's message in *Parsifal* would seem to be that there is no God, but that we have it within ourselves to redeem our lives if we cherish and follow certain aspects of Christ's teaching, as dramatized in the opera.

Personally, I would not interpret *Parsifal* in this way. I would leave open at least the possibility that within it there is a sense of a divine redemption, and hence a divinity, but even granted that, there would still be a huge difference between Wagner's myth or myths and the religious myths we have been focusing on in this essay. According to Roger Scruton, what Wagner is doing in his mythological operas is to make available to us in a non-religious age religious experience detached from religious belief. In order to do this, he draws on "those moments of unconscious knowledge that shine in the darkness of the old Teutonic poems. The point of lifting these moments from the myths was not to explain them, but to bring them to life, to convey their untranslatable spiritual meaning, and to incorporate them into a drama in which character and action take on an engaging and believable form."[15]

Let us accept that in a certain sense in Wagner's works the myths are brought to life, but they are brought to life on a stage, in a modern theatre. The whole context and atmosphere is quite different from participation in a religious ritual. Even though Wagner somewhat pretentiously referred to *Parsifal* as a sacred stage festival, attending a performance of it and his other operas is hardly conducive to the sense of reverence and humble awe that one would experience in even the most modest church service, or indeed that one is part of a venerable tradition and community or church. Even if there are ritualistic aspects to stage performances, as

---

15. Scruton, *The Ring of Truth*, 34.

Wagner would no doubt urge in the case of his works, they are not religiously ritualistic. In particular, they are not calls to observant behavior, to a directing of one's life in a given religious community in the way that religiously charged myths are. Even the most pharisaical and worldly worshipper in a church will occasionally feel that there is something wrong with his life. But I doubt that anyone leaving the Royal Opera House, or even Bayreuth, feels as a result of what they have seen that there is something wrong with his or her life, and immediately embraces the unprepossessing vagrant he or she is about to brush past in the street outside. In contrast to religious myths, whatever Wagner hoped or intended, the Wagnerian myths are not in a clear sense foundational to "ways of living," to revert our earlier reference to Wittgenstein. Maybe things were different in ancient Greece, and adherents left the theatre filled with divinely inspired emotion and resolve, but in ancient Greece, in contrast to a Wagnerian sacred stage festival, the plays *were* part of a full-blooded religious festival, a worshipping of the god Dionysus in the midst of a community of like-minded adepts.

As far as our other modern mythmakers go, Yeats seems to me to dabble in half-remembered myths and to weave poetry out of this dabbling, rather than actually create a new myth. In any case, his dabbling is just too idiosyncratic to form the basis of anything would-be followers might think to practice. Lewis and Tolkien did create powerful and coherent mythical stories, but in both cases what they created derives from and points us back to a very important myth that already exists and has done for two millennia. In so far as the myths woven by Tolkien and Lewis go, there is a religious community in which they are embedded, but it is the community of Christianity, which already has its venerable rituals and practices.

Rather than continuing to delve into modern mythmaking, at this point it would be enough to recall the belief of Gemistus Plethon that the *koina dogmata*, the fundamental beliefs, of all religions, as encapsulated in their myths, and behind and below those myths, are the same. Plethon, unsurprisingly, follows Plato in thinking that truth was purest at the beginning: "the sages always hold opinions that agree with older beliefs, so that, even by their age, the true doctrines are superior to the false, . . . whereas sophists always aim for something new."[16] I will end simply by saying that if we are to make any sense of what Ficino and Plethon are telling us about the commonality beneath the variety of the religious myths we discover throughout the world and throughout history, we must treat those myths imaginatively, as truths mirroring, often in oblique ways, a complex, transcendent, and partly inaccessible divine. In doing so, they also lead us into ways of acting and feeling, in community with others who are living within the same vision. We should refrain from looking at them as if they were merely anthropological exhibits or, even worse, would-be factual reports of a proto-scientific type. Such reports are indeed not the end of the matter.

---

16. Quoted in Wind, *Pagan Mysteries*, 245–46.

Bibliography

Aquinas, Thomas. *Summa Contra Gentiles*. Translated by A. C. Pegis. Notre Dame, IN: Notre Dame University Press, 1975.
———. *Summa Theologiae*. Edited by T. Gilby. London: Eyre and Spottiswode, 1963-75.
Aristotle. *Works of Aristotle*. Edited by J. Barnes. Princeton: Princeton University Press, 1984.
Armstrong, K. *Sacred Nature: How We Can Recover Our Bond with Nature*. London: The Bodley Head, 2022.
Augustine. "Commentary on Psalm 85." *Corpus Christianorum* 39 (1956) 1176-77.
———. *Retractions*. Translated by M. Bogan. Fathers of the Church, vol. 60. Washington, DC: Catholic University Press of America, 1968.
Ayer, A. J. *Language, Truth and Logic*. London: Gollancz, 1936.
Bloom, A. "The Crisis of Liberal Education." In *Giants and Dwarves: Essays 1960-1990*, 348-64. New York: Touchstone, 1991.
Bloom, P. *Berlioz in Time: From Early Recognition to Lasting Fame*. New York: University of Rochester Press, 2022.
Burke, E. *Reflections on the Revolution in France*. Edited by C. C. O'Brien. Harmondsworth, UK: Penguin, 1986.
Bushnell, H. *God in Christ*. New York: Schribner's Sons, 1877.
Calvin, J. *Psalms 93-150*. Calvin's Commentaries VII. Edinburgh: Calvin Translation Society, 1848.
Carloni, P. *Come in uno specchio*. Rome: Ginevra Bentivoglio EditoriA, 2019.
Carpenter, H. *J. R. R. Tolkien: A Biography*. London: Allen and Unwin, 1977.
Clooney, F. "Beyond My God, with God's Blessing." In *Philosophers and God: At the Frontiers of Faith and Reason*, edited by J. Cornwell and M. McGhee, 87-96. London: Continuum, 2009.
Cottingham, J. *Philosophy of Religion*. New York: Cambridge University Press, 2014.
Curry, O. S., D. A. Mullins, and H. Whitehouse. "Is It Good to Co-operate? Testing the Theory of Morality as Co-operation in 60 Societies." *Current Anthropology* 60.1 (2019) 47-69.

Bibliography

Dante, Alighieri. *Divine Comedy*. Bi-lingual ed. Translated by J. D. Sinclair. New York: Oxford University Press, 1961.

Darwin, F., ed. *The Life and Letters of Charles Darwin*. Vol. 1. New York: Appleton, 1897.

Descartes, R. *The Philosophical Writings of Descartes*. Edited by J. Cottingham, R. Stoothoff, and D. Murdoch. Cambridge: Cambridge University Press, 1985.

Dodds, E. R. *The Greeks and the Irrational*. Berkeley: University of California Press, 1971.

Engelmann, P. *Letters from Ludwig Wittgenstein, with a Memoir*. Translated by L. Furtmüller. Oxford: Blackwell, 1967.

Ficino, M. *Opera Omnia*. Enghien, Belgium: Les Éditions de Miraval, 2000.

Fisch, M., and D. Band. *Qohelet: Searching for a Life Worth Living*. Waco, TX: Baylor University Press, 2023.

Frazer, J. *The Golden Bough: A Study in Magic and Religion*. Abridged ed. London: Macmillan, 1922.

Garrow, D., and N. Wilkin, eds. *The World of Stonehenge*. London: British Museum Press, 2022.

Goethe, J. W. von. "Aphorisms on Art and Art History." In *German Aesthetics and Art History: The Romantic Ironists and Goethe*, edited by K. Wheeler, 226–36. Cambridge: Cambridge University Press, 1984.

Goodman, N. *The Structure of Appearance*. Cambridge: Harvard University Press, 1951.

Hacker, P. M. S. "Wittgenstein and the Autonomy of Humanistic Understanding." In *Wittgenstein, Theory and the Arts*, edited by R. Allen and M. Turvey, 39–74. London: Routledge, 2001.

Hadot, P. *Philosophy as a Way of Life*. Oxford: Blackwell, 1995.

Hankins, J. "The Significance of Renaissance Philosophy." In *The Cambridge Companion to Renaissance Philosophy*, edited by J. Hankins, 338–45. Cambridge: Cambridge University Press, 2007.

Hedley, D. *Coleridge, Philosophy and Religion: Aids to Reflection and the Mirror of the Spirit*. Cambridge: Cambridge University Press, 2000.

———. *Sacrifice Imagined: Violence, Atonement and the Sacred*. London: Continuum, 2011.

Heller, E. *The Disinherited Mind*. New York: Meridian, 1959.

Herbert of Cherbury. *De Veritate*. 1624 and 1645. Translated by M. H. Carré. Bristol: Arrowsmith, 1937.

Hick, J. *An Interpretation of Religion*. London Macmillan, 1980.

Hill, G. *Orchards of Syon*. London: Penguin, 2002.

Hughes, T. "Myth and Education." *Times Educational Supplement*, September 2, 1977.

Hume, D. *Dialogues Concerning Natural Religion*. Edited by D. Aitken. New York: Haffner, 1948.

Bibliography

Husserl, E. *The Crisis in the European Sciences and Transcendental Phenomenology.* Translated by D. Carr. Evanston, IL: Northwestern University Press, 1970.
Jones, D. *The Sleeping Lord and Other Fragments.* London: Faber and Faber, 1995.
Kant, I. *The Critique of Pure Reason.* Translated by N. Kemp Smith. London: Macmillan, 1963.
Kolakowski, L. *The Meaning of Myth.* Translated by A. Czerniawski. Chicago: Chicago University Press, 1989.
———. *Religion.* London: Fontana, 1982.
Larkin, P. *Collected Poems.* London: Faber and Faber, 1988.
Lewis, C. S. *The Abolition of Man.* London: Fount, 1999.
———. *An Experiment in Criticism.* Cambridge: Cambridge University Press, 1961.
———. "Myth Becomes Fact." In *God in the Dock: Essays in Theology and Ethics*, edited by W. Hooper, 54–60. Grand Rapids: Eerdmans, 1970.
Luchte, J. *Pythagoras and the Doctrine of Transmigration: Wandering Souls.* London: Continuum, 2009.
Lucretius. *On the Nature of the Universe.* Translated by R. E. Latham. Harmondsworth, UK: Penguin, 1971.
Macaulay, R. *The Towers of Trebizon.* London: Futura, 1981.
Mackie, J. L. *Ethics: Inventing Right and Wrong.* Harmondsworth, UK: Penguin, 1978.
McInerny, R. ed. *Aquinas: Selected Writings.* London: Penguin, 1998.
Montefiore, A. *Philosophy and the Human Paradox: Essays on Reason, Truth and Identity.* Edited by D. Sands. London: Routledge, 2020.
Morrisey, F. "Abd al-Karim al-Jili's Sufi View of Other Religions." *Mahgreb Review* 43.2 (2018) 175–89.
———. *A Short History of Islamic Thought.* London: Head of Zeus, 2021.
Nagel, T. *Mind and Cosmos: Why the Materialist Neo-Darwinian Conception of Nature Is Almost Certainly Wrong.* New York: Oxford University Press, 2012.
———. *The View from Nowhere.* Oxford: Oxford University Press, 1986.
Newman, John Henry. *Apologia Pro Vita Sua.* 1864. In *The Newman Reader.* Pittsburgh, PA: National Institute for Newman Studies, 2007. Online: https://www.newmanreader.org/works/apologia/index.html.
Nietzsche, F. *The Birth of Tragedy.* In *Basic Writings of Nietzsche*, edited by W. Kaufmann, 3–144. New York: Modern Library, 1968.
Peterson, J. *Maps of Meaning: The Architecture of Belief.* London: Routledge, 1999.
———. "Three Forms of Meaning and the Management of Complexity." Unpublished paper, 2013.
Phillips, D. Z. "Pictures of Eternity." In *D. Z. Phillips' Contemplative Philosophy of Religion*, edited by A. F. Sanders, 75–93. London: Routledge, 2016.

Bibliography

Plato. *The Collected Dialogues*. Edited by E. Hamilton and H. Cairns. Princeton: Princeton University Press, 1978.

———. *The Republic*. Translated by R. Waterfield. Oxford: Oxford University Press, 1993.

Popper, K. R. *Conjectures and Refutations*. 3rd ed. London: Routledge and Kegan Paul, 1969.

———. *Quantum Theory and the Schism in Physics*. London: Hutchinson, 1982.

Quine, W. V. O. "On What There Is." In *From a Logical Point of View*, 1–19. New York: Harper Torchbooks, 1963.

Rilke, R. M. *Duino Elegies*. Translated by J. B. Leishman and S. Spender. London: Chatto and Windus, 1975.

Robichaud, D. J-J. *Plato's Persona: Marsilio Ficino, Renaissance Humanism and the Platonic Triad*. Philadelphia: University of Pennsylvania Press, 2018.

Runciman, S. *Mistra: Byzantine Capital of the Peloponnese*. London: Thames and Hudson, 1980.

Ruskin, J. *The Bible of Amiens*. In *The Complete Works of John Ruskin*, edited by E. T. Cook and A. Wedderburn, vol. 33. London: George Allen, 1908.

———. *The Stones of Venice*. In *The Complete Works of John Ruskin*, edited by E. T. Cook and A. Wedderburn, vols. 9–11. London: George Allen, 1903.

Scruton, R. *The Ring of Truth*. London: Allen Lane, 2016.

———. *The Soul of the World*. Princeton: Princeton University Press, 2014.

Seferis, G. *A Poet's Journal: Days of 1945–51*. Translated by A. Anagnostopuolos. Cambridge: Belnap Press of the University of Harvard, 1974.

Swiatecka, M. J. *The Idea of the Symbol: Some Nineteenth Century Comparisons with Coleridge*. Cambridge: Cambridge University Press, 1980.

Tolkien, J. R. R. "On Fairy Stories." In *Monsters and the Critics and Other Essays*, edited by C. Tolkien, 106–61. London; George Allen and Unwin, 1988.

Turnbull, C. *The Mountain People*. New York: Simon and Schuster, 1972.

Verdon, T. "Christianity, the Renaissance and the Study of History." In *Christianity and the Renaissance*, edited by T. Verdon and J. Henderson, 1–37. Syracuse, NY: Syracuse University Press, 1990.

Vidler, A. *A Variety of Catholic Modernists*. Cambridge: Cambridge University Press, 1970.

Wagner, R. "Religion und Kunst." In *Gessamelte Schriften und Dichtungen*. Vol. 10. Leipzig: Fritzsche, 1880.

Weil, S. *The Need for Roots*. Translated by A. F. Wills. London: Ark, 1987.

Wilson, A. N. *Confessions: A Life of Failed Promises*. London: Bloomsbury, 2022.

———. *C. S. Lewis: A Biography*. London: Collins, 1999.

Winch, P. "Picture and Representation." *Tijdscrift voor filosophie* 49.1 (1987) 3–20.

Wind, Edgar. *Pagan Mysteries of the Renaissance*. Rev. ed. New York: Norton, 1969.

Wittgenstein, L. *Culture and Value*. Translated by P. Winch. Oxford: Blackwell, 1980.

BIBLIOGRAPHY

———. *Notebooks, 1914-1916*. Translated by G. E. M. Anscombe. Oxford: Blackwell, 1969.
———. *Philosophical Investigations*. Translated by G. E. M. Anscombe. Oxford: Blackwell, 1967.
———. "Remarks on Frazer's *Golden Bough*." *Human World* 3 (1971) 18-41.
———. *Tractatus Logico-Philosophicus*. Translated by D. F. Pears and B. F. McGuinness. London: Routledge and Kegan Paul, 1963.

Index

Achilles, 30
Adam, 96
Adler, Alfred, 58
Adonis, 50, 53, 55, 76, 82, 124
Aeschylus, 123
Aglaophamus, 118
Alberich (dwarf), 128
Alighieri, Dante. See Dante Alighieri
al-Jili, Abd al-Karim, 103, 103n13, 105
Amelius, 118, 122
Anaximander, 59
Aphrodite, 97. See also Venus
Apollo, 43, 126
Apsu (god), 35
Aquinas, Thomas, St., 19–20, 20n15, 21, 40, 41, 88, 95, 103–4, 109, 115n1, 117, 118n6
Aristotle, 39, 125
Armstrong, Karen, 38, 38n6
Arnold, Matthew, 127
Athena, 75n2
Attis, 82
Augustine, of Hippo, St., 42, 44, 44n11, 117, 117n5
Augustus, emperor, 33
Ayer, A. J., 13, 25

Bacchus, 43, 50, 53, 76, 124. See also Dionysus

Bach, Johann Sebastian, 45
Balder (Baldr), 50, 53, 55, 76, 124, 124n10
Band, D., 89n3
Barbier, Auguste, 47
Berlioz, Hector, 47
Bloom, Allan, 126, 126n12
Bloom, P., 47n19
Bohr, Niels, 106, 107n17
Botticelli, Sandro, 97
Bradwardine, Thomas, 124n10
Brünnhilde (daughter of Wotan), 128
Buddha, 93n7. See also Gautama
Burckhardt, Jacob, 115
Burke, Edmund, 91
Bushnell, Horace, 106, 107n16
Byron, George Gordon, Lord, 20

Calvin, John, 40, 40n9
Caravaggio, Michelangelo Merisi, 98, 99
Carloni, Paolo, 55n6
Carpenter, Hiumphrey, 111n20
Chopin, Frédéric, 45
Cleanthes, 115n1
Clooney, Francis, 104, 105n15, 109
Coleridge, Samuel Taylor, 20, 63, 80–81, 81n6
Colet, John, 101n12, 116
Colonna, Vittoria, 55, 55n6

Index

Cottingham, John, 112, 112n21
Curry, O. S., 75n2

Dalton, John, 61, 62, 63
Dante Alighieri, 54, 79, 87, 90, 102, 119
Darwin, Charles, 67
Darwin, F., 68n9
Davidson, Donald, 45
Dawkins, Richard, 76
Democritus, 60, 61, 62
Dennett, Daniel, 76
Descartes, René, 111, 112, 113
Dionysus, 43, 55, 90. *See also* Bacchus
Dodds, E. R., 44, 44n10
Dostoyevsky, Fyodor, 95
Dvorak, Antonín, 51
Dyson, Hugo, 49

Egidio de Viterbo, 90
Eliot, T. S., 127
Empedocles, 59, 66, 126
Engelmann, Paul, 15, 15n8
Epicurus, 60, 61, 62
Erasmus, 101n12
Euripides, 43, 123
Ezekiel, 100–101

Faust, 90–91, 109
Ficino, Marsilio, 56, 90, 101n12, 116, 116n3, 121–22, 122n7, 123–24, 123n9, 125, 126, 131
Fisch, Menachem, 89, 89n3
Foxe, John, 101n12
Frazer, James, 16, 32
Frege, Gottlob, 11
Freud, Sigmund, 58

Gaia, 97, 98
Galileo, 108
Garin, Eugenio, 108n18
Garrow, D., 37n4
Gautama, 94. *See also* Buddha
Goethe, Johann Wolfgang von, 81, 81n6, 90, 109

Goodman, Nelson, 13, 25
Gould, Glenn, 45
Greeves, Arthur, 105

Hacker, Peter (P. M. S.), 17, 17n12, 18, 21, 85, 110
Hades, 59
Hadot, Pierre, 70, 70n11
Hamlet, 46
Hankins, J., 116n3
Hébert, Marcel, 104, 104n14
Hecuba, 46
Hedley, Douglas, 66, 66n8, 81n6
Heidegger, Martin, 7, 8
Heller, Erich, 78–79, 78n3
Heraclitus, 59, 98
Herbert, George, 71, 71n1
Herbert of Cherbury, Edward, 71–74, 92
Hermes, 118, 125
Hick, John, 92–93, 92n6, 94, 94n9, 110
Hill, Geoffrey, 93, 93n8
Holbein, Hans, the Younger, 95
Homer, 37, 38, 58, 75n2, 123
Hopkins, Gerard Manley, 98
Horace, 75n2
Hughes, Ted, 29, 29n1
Hulewicz, Witold von, 78
Hume, David, 25, 26, 28, 115n1
Husserl, Edmund, 26

Iamblichus, 118
Ibn al-A'rabi, 102–3, 103n13, 105
Isis, 82

Jesus Christ, 33, 42, 43, 44, 49, 53, 54, 55, 56, 87, 94, 95, 104, 117, 118, 119, 123, 124, 129
Jones, David, 87–88, 88n1
Josephus, 33
Jove, 75n2. *See also* Zeus
Julius Caesar, 49

Kant, Immanuel, 19, 19n14, 20, 21–22, 24, 105

Index

Keats, John, 80, 80n4
Kolakowski, L., 32n2, 38n7

Lao Tzu, 38
Larkin, Philip, 61, 61n5
Lavoisier, Antoine, 63
Leibniz, Gotfried Wilhelm, 39
Leucippus, 60, 61, 62
Lewis, C. S., 38, 38n8, 48–50, 52, 53, 55, 56, 69, 75, 75n2, 76, 80, 80n5, 91, 92, 94–95, 94n10, 105, 109, 110, 111, 111n20, 124, 124n10, 127, 130
Luchte, James, 122n8
Lucretius, 61, 61n6, 62

Macaulay, Rose, 101n12
Mackie, J. L., 122n7
Mahler, Gustav, 125
Malatesta, Sigismondo, 117n4
Manfred (medieval warrior), 79
Marduk (god), 36
Mars, 75n2
Marshall, Perry, 88n2
Marta (friend of Peter, *Anna* opera), 50
Matthews, David, 50, 50n2
Mawson, Tim, 124n10
Maxwell, James Clerk, 63
McInerny, Ralph, 20, 20n16
Medea, 128
Medici, Lorenzo de,' 115
Michelangelo, 54, 55, 55n6, 96, 98, 99, 118–21
Montefiore, Alan, 88n2
More, Thomas, 101n12, 116
Morrissey, Fitzroy, 103n13
Muhammad, 33, 64, 84, 94, 103, 105
Mullins, D. A., 75n2

Nagel, Thomas, 24, 68, 68n10
Newman, John Henry, St., 101, 101n12, 102
Nietzsche, Friedrich, 48, 48n15

Noah, 103

Oedipus, 82
Orpheus, 43, 118, 125, 126
Osiris, 82
Ouranos, 97, 98. *See also* Uranus

Parmenides, 59
Parsifal (human knight), 129
Pascal, Blaise, 46, 73, 76, 106
Paul, St., 42, 54, 55, 98, 99, 122. *See also* Saul of Tarsus
Persephone, 43
Peter, St., 54, 55
Peter (character, *Anna* opera), 50
Peterson, Jordan, 36, 36n3, 44, 44n12, 46
Phaedra, 128
Phillips, D. Z., 96, 96n11
Pico della Mirandola, Giovanni, 108, 108n18
Pius X, St., Pope, 104, 105
Plato, 42, 54, 56, 73, 91, 97, 101n12, 112, 115, 116, 117n4, 118, 122, 122n8, 123n9, 124, 125, 126, 127, 130
Plethon, Gemistus, 116n3, 117, 117n4, 125, 130–31
Plotinus, 117, 117n4, 118
Popper, Karl R., 57–58, 57n1, 58n2, 59–60, 59n3, 60n4, 66–67, 69, 70, 89, 106, 107n17
Porphyry, 118
Poseidon, 59
Prajapati (god), 43
Proclus, 118
Protagoras, 122
Pseudo-Dionysius, 122
Pythagoras, 59, 66, 115, 118, 126

Quine, W. V. O., 13, 13n5

Rahner, Karl, 106
Raine, Kathleen, 110

Index

Raphael, 100
Rembrandt, 47
Rilke, Ranier Maria, 63, 63n7, 64, 77–78
Robichaud, D. J-J., 116n3, 117n4, 122n7, 122n8, 123n9, 124n10, 126n11
Rorty, Richard, 76
Runciman, Steven, 117n4
Ruskin, John, 75n2, 84–86, 84n10
Russell, Bertrand, 7, 8, 10, 11, 14, 15

Santa Claus, 84
Sartre, Jean-Paul, 7, 8, 76
Saul of Tarsus, 54, 98, 99. See also Paul
Schelling, Friedrich Wilhelm Joseph, 63, 64
Schiller, Friedrich, 57
Schlegel, Friedrich, 69, 81
Schlick, Moritz, 12
Schumann, Robert, 45, 69
Scruton, Roger, 50, 50n2, 51–52, 52n4, 82, 82n9, 129, 129n15
Seferis, George, 37, 37n5, 127, 127n13
Shakespeare, William, 47
Sieglinde, 128
Smetana, Bedřich, 51
Socrates, 49, 125–26
Sokolov, Grigory, 45
Sophia, 97
Swiatecka, M. Jadwiga, 82, 82n8

Talich, Václac, 51n3
Tarski, Alfred, 45
Thales, 59

Theodore (Neoplatonist), 118
Thomas, D. M., 29
Thucydides, 123
Tiamat (goddess), 35
Tolkien, J. R. R., 35, 48–50, 53, 56, 69, 80, 91, 111, 111n20, 127, 130
Turnbull, Colin, 75n2

Uranus, 97. See also Ouranos

Venus, 97. See also Aphrodite
Verdon, Timothy, 115, 116, 116n2
Vidler, Alec, 104n14

Wagner, Richard, 35, 51, 127–30, 128n14
Weil, Simone, 115, 116n2, 123
Whitehouse, H., 75n2
Wilkin, N., 37n4
Wilson, A. N., 49, 49n1, 56n7, 101n12, 111n19
Winch, Peter, 81, 81n7
Wind, Edgar, 90n4, 108n18, 116n3, 117n4
Wittgenstein, Ludwig, 7–12, 8nn1–2, 11n3, 12n4, 13, 14–17, 14n6, 15n7, 15n9, 16nn10–11, 18, 18n13, 21, 21n17, 23, 24, 44, 44n13, 45, 48, 79, 106, 125, 127, 130
Wotan (ruling god), 128
Wynn, Mark, 77

Yeats, W. B., 78, 127, 130

Zeus, 59. See also Jove
Zoroaster, 118, 125

www.ingramcontent.com/pod-product-compliance
Lightning Source LLC
Chambersburg PA
CBHW031500160426
43195CB00010BB/1050